DATE DUE

First American Art

First American Art

THE CHARLES AND VALERIE DIKER COLLECTION
OF AMERICAN INDIAN ART

EDITED BY

Bruce Bernstein

Gerald McMaster

ESSAYS BY

Bruce Bernstein

Gerald McMaster

Margaret Dubin

Donald Kuspit

CAPTIONS COMPILED BY

Kathleen Ash-Milby

Smithsonian
National Museum of the American Indian

Washington, D.C., and New York

in association with

University of Washington Press
Seattle and London

Published in conjunction with the exhibition *First American Art: The Charles and Valerie Diker Collection of American Indian Art*, on view at the Smithsonian's National Museum of the American Indian, George Gustav Heye Center, Alexander Hamilton U.S. Custom House, New York City, 24 April 2004– 31 October 2005.

NMAI Head of Publications: Terence Winch
Editor, NMAI: Elizabeth Kennedy Gische

The Smithsonian's National Museum of the American Indian is dedicated to working in collaboration with the indigenous peoples of the Americas to protect and foster Native cultures throughout the Western Hemisphere. The museum's publishing program seeks to augment awareness of Native American beliefs and lifeways, and to educate the public about the history and significance of Native cultures. For information about the Smithsonian's National Museum of the American Indian, visit the NMAI Website at www.AmericanIndian.si.edu.

University of Washington Press
P.O. Box 50096
Seattle, WA 98145-5096
www.washington.edu/uwpress

Edited by Catherine Steinmann
Proofread by Laura Iwasaki and Carrie Wicks
Indexed by Sherry Smith
Designed by John Hubbard
Composition by Marie Weiler with assistance by Ken Ligda
Object photography by Dirk Bakker
Color separations by iocolor, Seattle
Produced by Marquand Books, Inc., Seattle
   www.marquand.com
Printed and bound by C&C Offset Printing Co., Ltd., China

Front cover: **Rattle**, c. 1780, artist unknown, Tsimshian; wood, hair, bone, nails, pigment, sinew, rattling material, 37 × 20 × 14 cm, DAC 664 (cat. no. 112). Front cover and page 54: **Coin bowl**, c. 1820, Lapulimeu, Chumash; dyed and undyed juncus stems, 18 × 47 cm, DAC 522 (cat. no. 8).

Back cover: **Blanket strip** (detail), c. 1830, artist unknown, Upper Missouri or Northern Plains; hide, glass beads, sinew, 26 × 170 × 3 cm, DAC 707 (cat. no. 56).

Page 1: **Bag** (detail), c. 1860, artist unknown, Wasco; cotton fabric, cotton thread, glass beads, hide, copper alloy buttons, beads, 74 × 18 × 5 cm, DAC 570 (cat. no. 168).

Frontispiece: **Olla**, c. 1770, artist unknown, Ako (Acoma); clay, slip, 28 × 31 cm, DAC 310 (cat. no. 5). **Bag**, c. 1800, artist unknown, Mississauga Ojibwe; hide, porcupine quills, silk, hair, tinned iron, vegetal cordage, glass beads, 35 × 27 × 4 cm, DAC 586 (cat. no. 14). **Baby moccasins**, c. 1830, artist unknown, Cheyenne; hide, glass beads, sinew, pigment, 7 × 6 × 13 cm each, DAC 573 (cat. no. 13). **Blanket strip**, c. 1865, artist unknown, Nez Perce(?); hide, glass beads, porcupine quill, copper alloy bells, wool, sinew, 15 × 160 × 3 cm, DAC 690 (cat. no. 22).

Library of Congress Cataloging-in-Publication Data
   First American art : the Charles and Valerie Diker collection of American Indian art / edited by Bruce Bernstein and Gerald McMaster; essays by Bruce Bernstein . . . [et al.].
      p. cm.
   "Published in conjunction with the exhibition First American art: The Charles and Valerie Diker collection of American Indian Art, on view at the Smithsonian's National Museum of the American Indian, George Gustav Heye Center, Alexander Hamilton U.S. Custom House, New York City, 24 April 2004–31 October 2005"—Prelim.
   Includes index.
   ISBN 0-295-98403-1 (hardcover : alk. paper) — ISBN 0-9719163-2-2 (softcover : alk. paper)
   1. Indian art—North America—Exhibitions. 2. Indians of North America—Material culture—Exhibitions. 3. Indians of North America—Antiquities—Collectors and collecting—Exhibitions. 4. Diker, Charles—Ethnological collections—Exhibitions. 5. Diker, Valerie—Ethnological collections—Exhibitions. 6. National Museum of the American Indian (U.S.). George Gustav Heye Center—Exhibitions. I. Bernstein, Bruce. II. McMaster, Gerald. III. National Museum of the American Indian (U.S.). George Gustav Heye Center. IV. Alexander Hamilton United States Custom House (New York, N.Y.).
E98.A7F54 2004
704.03'97'0074753—dc22   2003026013

Contents

Foreword

ARTFUL VISION

To be truly distinguished at what they do, collectors must bring to their vocation a level of creativity commensurate with the work they are acquiring. A keen eye and a ready checkbook will take you only so far: a great collector must have a coherent vision as well. The collector who makes a difference is the one who kicks open the doors of perception by showing us techniques, ideas, and accomplishments we would perhaps not have observed on our own. I believe you will see in this book and its accompanying exhibition an inspirational example of great collecting on the part of Charles and Valerie Diker.

A time existed in our history when no one would think to call the cultural objects of Native peoples "art." That term was reserved for the efforts of "civilized" people only, those working according to the rules and regulations of Western aesthetics. With such closed and shortsighted attitudes now, I hope, forever abandoned, we can see quite clearly the immense accomplishments, in sheer aesthetic terms, of so much of Indian art. We have had to rethink our old assumptions. As the estimable art historian David Penney suggested a number of years ago, "It is now not so much the issue of defining American Indian creations to fit a European definition of 'art,' but of redefining 'art.'" We hope this book and exhibition will contribute something to that redefinition.

The works included here, from many tribal traditions across Canada and the United States, are manifestations of the cultures from which they spring; an awareness of this gives us an opportunity to understand what qualities contribute to their visual identity. At the National Museum of the American Indian (NMAI), we hold close the principle that Native objects must be placed in their complex cultural contexts if they are to be understood completely. But that is not to say that the aesthetic dimension of these masterworks should be given short shrift. *First American Art: The Charles and Valerie Diker Collection of American Indian Art* has provided us with the welcome opportunity to explore and celebrate the aesthetic achievements, creativity, and diverse artistic traditions of North American Native peoples. We hope that this project, by offering an aesthetic analysis of the underlying spiritual and cultural inspirations and values that inform these works, gives a more complete picture of what we mean by Native art.

Charles and Valerie Diker have long been generous supporters of the museum. That spirit of generosity extended to this project—not only have they lent us their superb collection, they also opened the doors of their home to the key contributors to this effort for days of brainstorming. Given the Dikers' long involvement with the museum, it seems fitting to me that we should extend our own welcome to their extraordinary collection of Native works; of course, they will feel very much at home in the George Gustav Heye Center, our New York facility, named for the collector, himself a New Yorker, who assembled our own vast collection.

Although this project grows out of many years of astute and passionate collecting by the Dikers, I also must cite our debt to NMAI curators Bruce Bernstein and Gerald McMaster (Plains Cree), whose vision for this book and exhibition energized all involved. I must acknowledge, too, Donald Kuspit and Margaret Dubin for their thoughtful essays, as well as the Native and non-Native artists, curators, and scholars who met to participate in vigorous discussions around the central subject: Arthur Amiotte (Lakota), Janet Berlo, J. J. Brody, Robert Davidson (Haida), Emil Her Many Horses (Lakota), Tom Hill (Seneca), Frank Ettawageshik (Odawa), Harry Fonseca (Maidu), Mary Jane Lenz, Truman Lowe (Ho-Chunk), Ann McMullen, and Peter Macnair. The work of guest assistant curator Kathleen Ash-Milby (Navajo) was indispensable to both the book and the exhibition, as was Betsy Shack's assistance on behalf of Charles and Valerie Diker. Kerry Boyd and Peter Brill, along with Susanna Stieff, Dominique Cocuzza, Rachel Griffin, Rajshree Solanki, Stacey Jones, John Richardson, and Geoffrey Cavanagh, have also provided invaluable support for the project. NMAI project manager Lindsay Stamm Shapiro coordinated the large cast of skilled people necessary to produce a major exhibition. Imrey-Culbert Architects Atelier gave life to the collection through their exhibition design. Dirk Bakker took the wonderful object photographs that appear in these pages, Catherine Steinmann patiently and sensitively edited the text, and Marquand Books, working with NMAI Publications head Terence Winch and editor Elizabeth Kennedy Gische, produced this handsome volume.

W. Richard West
(Southern Cheyenne and member of the
Cheyenne and Arapaho tribes of Oklahoma)
Director

First American Art

ART EVOKES EMOTIONS THAT AFFECT ALL OUR SENSES. IT IS A MOMENT MADE VISIBLE
and accessible by the artist. The emotional is made intellectual when the artist decides on materials and
technique or when the viewer wants to know about the object's meaning or content. More often, we "get"
it and have an emotional reaction to or an exclamation of recognition of something that has crawled into
our heads and created a solid experience, vision, or feeling; this is an aesthetic experience. In essence, both
artist and observer become one, sharing, for that brief instant, an understanding of the world. When art is
just right, it provides clarity, or perhaps an unanticipated beauty, that reminds us of who we are. If the artist
does his or her work well, we may gasp, acknowledging that there are shared visions and understandings.
This highly unscientific but nonetheless reliable "gasp factor" makes for a useful measurement. As Maidu
artist Harry Fonseca suggests, "The gasp is good enough; we don't need to explain it further."

What is perhaps less clear is how we identify good art, especially since art can be so enmeshed in the
artist's culture and personal background that we, as observers, may find it inaccessible. Particular notions of
beauty and content are culturally specific. Given this, if we had insights into a culture's notions of beauty,
could we understand or find more beauty in its art? Confusing the notion of art further is the question: Is
the idea of art universal? If we agree here that art is universal not in its particulars but rather in its broad
meanings, then we could certainly suggest that good art speaks with clarity of tone and purpose. It might
follow that an emotional reaction to art is transcultural. Can an observer across another culture experience
the same gasp? If so, is that person emoting over the same vision the artist believed he or she was making?

For decades, art produced by American Indian people has been discussed around the simple question: Is
it art? Is it art when it is understandable and accessible only to Indian people? European-American society's
relationship with and understanding of the alterity (otherness) of non-European cultures have often been
uneasy; this has frequently meant that art made by Indian artists has been relegated to museums of ethnography and natural history or discussed in special (marginal) sections in art historical studies and art museums,
usually because it was believed to be without an aesthetic discourse. An anthropological or art historical

Opposite: *Jar* (detail), c. 1790, artist unknown, Chumash;
sumac, dyed and undyed juncus, 17 × 24 cm, DAC 363
(cat. no. 36).

Hania katsina, c. 1890, artist unknown, Hopi; wood, cotton, wool, feathers, tinned iron, hide, pigment, 41 × 17 × 14 cm, DAC 317 (cat. no. 34). *Pahlik' mana katsina*, c. 1890, artist unknown, Hopi; wood, feathers, shell, pigment, cordage, 41 × 26 × 10 cm, DAC 198 (cat. no. 30).

approach to a Northern Plains man's shirt, for example, will often be entirely different: while the anthropologist uses the shirt to talk about human culture, the art museum will be more interested in displaying its formalistic qualities, its beauty. Both approaches are valid, but both will probably ignore the idea that the shirt was originally conceptualized and created within its own system of critique. To argue about whether or not it is art doesn't bring us any closer to a recognition of its particular values. What may bring us closer to that understanding is to consider whether an American Indian aesthetic exists, and, if so, what the criteria are for understanding it.

It is this idea of an indigenous system of aesthetics and art that this project seeks to explicate. We believe that you, the observer, will gain an improved appreciation of the art through understanding a system of Native exegesis. Our firm conviction is that we should acknowledge and articulate existing epistemological systems rather than create new ones, seeking to keep the artwork alive through making connections to Native cultures and intellectualism. We fully believe we can do this by stripping away what others

have said about Native art and returning to the original identity of the object—freed of the shackles of analysis and categorization—to help us see the art itself rather than what others may want us to see. By shaking loose chimerical pre-determinations such as the notion of an authentic Indian art, or that Indian art is traditional, or that real Indian art is made by Indians for Indians—we can better see and appreciate the object in front of us.

The National Museum of the American Indian is committed to presenting art from the viewpoint of the inherent and indigenous systems of aesthetics that guided its creation, from the choice of materials to the slope of the brow on a mask or the silhouette of a bowl. There are profound insights to be gained into art by seeing it through the eyes of its makers. It is the work of the museum to point out and explicate the intellectual and cultural systems that are used by Native artists in the creation of their art. By paying attention to these Native aesthetic systems, we seek to heighten our understanding and appreciation, not to undo any past forms of appreciation. Our intent here is to uncover existing systems of analysis rather than impose new ones. Art is material that speaks not for itself but through the tastes, interests, values, politics, and state of knowledge of its presenters.

Fundamental to American Indian aesthetics is a body of intellectual precepts and knowledge that was created by and continues to affect Native people and their cultures, which are wholly separate from and independent of the numerous outside cultures that have settled in the Americas. Certainly indigenous cultures have adopted and continue to adopt and incorporate new materials and ideas; these cultural changes maintain and keep Native cultures vibrant and vital. As a Pueblo friend tells us, this is the "persistence and insistence" of Native life. In the Native world, certain materials, techniques, and ideas are a fundamental part of aesthetics. For example, an object made of porcupine quills decorating a piece of buffalo hide uses materials, techniques, and ideas wholly indigenous to North America. Nonetheless, glass beads manufactured in Europe were quickly adapted and accepted because the art form was dynamic; beads easily fit into existing patterns and understandings. This of course does not take away from what was probably the elation of finding new materials and techniques to evolve and expand art and its work of capturing and explaining the world that surrounds us. Across time, good art continues to evoke the excitement of expanding worlds and possibilities.

In *First American Art*, we will come to know these aesthetic systems as articulated by artists, scholars, and collectors. Some of the artists speak about received perspectives on how their work is influenced by ancestral works. The late Tlingit artist James Schoppert once described his own influences by comparing the artist to the hunter: "The more one knew of his world the more successful he would be in the hunt. The same holds true for the Native artist who carves."[1] Chiricahua Apache sculptor Bob Haozous, who has a rather sly way of looking at historical influences, says: "I use international concepts that the Europeans attributed to Native Americans . . . that certainly are not true today, but did give a foundation, however questionable, on which to base my art."[2] Like so many contemporary Native artists, Schoppert and Haozous are products of their cultures; they have lived, studied, created, and contributed to them. Often their knowledge is built on the foundation of the historical legacy of old objects, not to replicate or copy, but rather to understand and explicate their ideology, values, beliefs, and attitudes. Schoppert says about creating masks based on old forms: "I did them just to learn the basics of masks, but they never looked real traditional."[3] Scholars and artists, Native and non-Native, bring their perspectives as practiced through years of research and writing, of comparing one object with another, of seeing many collections around the world, and of presenting new theories and ideas of historic Native art. Through these artists, scholars, and collectors, the museum visitor will come to know and understand these aesthetic systems and the ways Native people see the world through their objects.

Our purpose here is to describe art through Native voice, using the notions of authority, perspective, and visuality to gain insight. Today many Native scholars are emerging, taking their places alongside the non-Native voices that have long dominated the discourse on Indian art. We believe that the inclusion of Native scholars and artists in the discussion can foreground the Native voice and help bring a new perspective on subjects that have in the past been extensively written about and researched by others.

The voice of authority has generally been non-Indian, because it was believed that Indians couldn't speak for themselves in an objective way and that their views needed to be filtered, synthesized, or articulated by outsiders. Indian people were regarded as, using the derogatory term, mere "informants." Native-made art was also sometimes interpreted as "primitive art," belonging to a stage of civilization through which Western cultures had already evolved. It was in this way not understood or studied as an art system, but rather as part of an evolutionary framework. As various tribes began to assert their rights to self-determination and positioned themselves as sovereign bodies, they have increasingly become the acknowledged owners and keepers of their cultural heritage with authority over how it was to be presented.

Exhibitions such as *First American Art* can add individual or tribal perspectives to an already diverse body of scholarship on the subject of Indians. Various perspectives will interpret an art object as commodity, artifact, specimen, heirloom, objet d'art, treasured cultural heritage, or sacred emblem. What would be the Native perspective? This is a question this exhibition attempts to address. The collector who purchases a work as an objet d'art will present it from that perspective. The original owners or makers will certainly have had a different perspective on its meaning, as will contemporary Indian artists.

While *perspective* concerns abstract ideas, *visuality* concerns the visible and tangible; the two are closely related. Creating an art object or designing an exhibition is never an innocent or unbiased project; it is never without a cultural perspective. The way we see the world is influenced by many factors, including language, geography, education, family, and community. Visuality relates to the contexts of the artist and his or her culture and influences.

A confluence of good forces came together to allow us to explore these issues. The extraordinary opportunity to produce this catalogue and exhibition was provided by Charles and Valerie Diker. Many of us in the academic, museum, and art worlds have striven over the years to elevate discussions of Indian art to the level of art. The Dikers too have hoped to help people appreciate the beauty and possibilities of art made by Native people by freeing them of the idea that if an object is Indian made, it must be either ethnography or part of a category separate from and unequal to European or American art. We are not the first to consider or speak about these issues, nor will we be the last. This exhibition and catalogue mark a cumulative moment in an ongoing shift in which people are coming to enjoy the art rather than to learn about Indians. To enjoy the art is to seek and gain insight about its internal presence. The Dikers collect modern and contemporary art; indeed, in their New York apartment, Native American art sits comfortably beside and in juxtaposition to non-Native art. Their love is of the beautiful object, the objet d'art. Having collected art as their keen aesthetic eye has directed them, with little regard to traditional categories of segregation, they have committed themselves to changing perceptions. They have also challenged the National Museum of the American Indian to rise to a more prominent role in this discussion.

As co-curators, we knew that we could not possibly take on this task ourselves and that we needed to consult some of the Native and non-Native scholars and artists who have been at the forefront of such discussions over the past few decades. We believed there was no better place to meet than in the heart of the Dikers' collection, in their home, surrounded by their unique melding of modern art with historical Indian art. Following initial awestruck appreciations of their artistic vision by the visiting curatorial group members, we sat at their dining room table for two days of discussions about the meanings of Native art. In the end, our seminar settled on seven principles of Native aesthetics—*idea, emotion, intimacy, movement, integrity, vocabulary,* and *composition*—carried in every Native object.

Our curatorial group was extraordinary. Our thanks go to Arthur Amiotte, Janet Berlo, J. J. Brody, Robert Davidson, Emil Her Many Horses, Tom Hill, Frank Ettawageshik, Harry Fonseca, Mary Jane Lenz, Truman Lowe, Peter Macnair, and Ann McMullen. Donald Kuspit and Margaret Dubin, our essayists, contributed good words and ideas to our collective. Kathleen Ash-Milby added her insights as well. In this catalogue and exhibition, which represent our combined experiences, we have attempted to summarize those conversations, articulating them according to the seven principles. Artists articulate these principles primarily through their work rather than through discussion and writing. It has been our intention to act as scribes to elucidate and make them accessible, to bring them forward, to create intelligibility through them. The work of organizing the collection around the principles has clarified them. We have classified each object according to the principle we believe it best illustrates; nonetheless, each object carries all seven of the principles.

In two days of free-ranging discussions, the members of our group managed to work as a cohesive body. While we are indebted to our colleagues for so willingly and openly sharing their insights and vast knowledge, we are responsible for our summations and organization of the two days of discussion into seven aesthetic principles. We have welcomed this collaborative effort to investigate something as ethereal as art and its meanings.

Bruce Bernstein
Gerald McMaster

Notes

1. "Give It Eyes and Teeth and I'll Buy It: The Native Artist in the '80s," in *Instrument of Change: Jim Schoppert Retrospective Exhibition, 1947–1992* (Anchorage Museum of History and Art, 1997), 32.

2. Quoted in Margaret Dubin, "Sanctioned Scribes: How Critics and Historians Write the Native American Art World," in W. Jackson Rushing, ed., *Native American Art in the Twentieth Century* (New York: Routledge, 1999), 159.

3. *Instrument of Change* (note 1), 8.

MARGARET DUBIN

Collecting

NATIVE AMERICAN ART
IN THE TWENTY-FIRST CENTURY

AMERICAN MUSEUMS HAVE BEEN DISPLAYING COLLECTIONS OF NATIVE AMERICAN ART for more than a century. During this time technology has grown more sophisticated, legal parameters have changed, and political contexts have shifted, but the objects have remained constant, for the most part, in both their appearance and their relationship to the audience. What would it take, the curators at the Smithsonian's National Museum of the American Indian (NMAI) recently asked themselves, to do something different? When Charles (Chuck) and Valerie Diker offered to put a large portion of their 350-piece collection of historical Native American art on display at the museum's George Gustav Heye Center in New York City, an opportunity to produce a different kind of exhibition presented itself.

While the Diker collection might not be unusual in its range of objects, its context is remarkable. Amassed over a thirty-year period, the collection was integrated into a large and visually arresting collection of modern American and European painting and sculpture. Throughout the Dikers' Manhattan home, Native American baskets, pots, and beaded blanket strips are creatively juxtaposed with paintings by the likes of Jim Dine, Joan Miró, and Robert Rauschenberg and with sculptures by Louise Nevelson and Alexander Calder. The juxtapositions aren't perfunctory or accidental; they reflect the collectors' universalist philosophy about art and their attitude toward Native American art in particular. The Dikers articulate their response to the Native American objects in the same language they use to speak about the modern art: "We are struck by their visual beauty." They speak of particular pieces being particularly striking because of their integrity, or because of their use of positive and negative space.

One of the goals of the NMAI is to enable the viewing public to see Native American objects as *art* instead of as *ethnological artifact*. Labels don't change the actual appearance of things, of course, but can change their meaning and value and, by doing so, change the way those objects are perceived. Just as artworks look different in their contexts of production—a blanket on a loom under a cottonwood tree on the Navajo reservation, or a paint-splattered canvas leaning against the wall of an artist's studio—and in their contexts of consumption—the blanket on a slanted display stand under a Plexiglas case in a museum, the

Opposite: *Tray* (detail), c. 1890, artist unknown,
Western Apache; willow, cottonwood, Martynia,
11 × 54 cm, DAC 395 (cat. no. 99).

Honor Song at Painted Tipi,
c. 1880, Julian Scott Ledger
Artist A, Kiowa; pencil, ink,
colored pencil, 19 × 31 cm,
DAC 057LD.

painting under a spotlight on a white art-gallery wall—the
labels used to describe and categorize objects can cause
them to be perceived differently. To call something "art"
is to associate it with high-status objects and an elite
discourse; to call the same thing "artifact" is to associate
it with the kinds of cultural relics found in middens by
archaeologists. The discourses surrounding these two broad
categories are real and factor heavily into our perceptions
and value judgments, but the notion that any one object
necessarily and always belongs in one category rather than
the other is false because categorization shifts depending
on the categorizer's intentions.

By presenting Native American art as "art," not "artifact," the NMAI hopes to encourage viewers to change
their perceptions of the status of Native American objects
and the artists who produce them. With the full support of
the Dikers, who share this goal, the museum's curators set
out to create an environment in which an exhibition could
be developed that would change viewers' relationship to
the objects. Not content to rely on the conventional art-
gallery strategies of white walls, individual Plexiglas cases,
and spotlights, the curators initiated a long-term project in
which Native and non-Native artists and scholars of Native
American art would be brought in as consultants to create a
new paradigm for museum interpretation and display.

Project co-curators Bruce Bernstein and Gerald
McMaster's first steps included identifying scholars and
artists to serve as consultants. Once selected, these consultants were invited to attend a two-day meeting to map
out their vision for the exhibition. The site of the meeting
was the Dikers' home, where the eight invited consultants,

along with museum staff, were surrounded by more varie-
ties of art in one set of rooms than probably many had ever
before experienced. In the foyer alone were paintings by
Chuck Close, Joan Miró, Ad Reinhardt, and April Gornick,
graceful Japanese baskets from the early twentieth century,
nineteenth-century Ainu tunics, and, in their midst, hanging
on a narrow, prominent outcropping of wall, a brilliant pink-
and-blue beaded Nez Perce blanket strip (cat. no. 22).

Things got off to a slow start, as participants were reluc-
tant to sit at the table when there was so much incredible art
to look at. The consultants wandered off alone or in small
groups to take it all in, while the Dikers—unfazed, patient,
and ready to answer questions—greeted latecomers. When
asked if they had had this many people in their apartment
before, the Dikers said yes, but that it had been "more of a
social thing." While most of the consultants were old friends
and colleagues and many had quite a bit of catching up to
do, the purpose for this meeting was business: the essential
emotional business of listening to each other articulate his
or her responses to Native American objects of their choos-
ing, and the difficult cerebral business of translating these
responses into a game plan for interpretation and display.
With a collection as sizable and of such high caliber as the
Dikers', the possibilities were endless.

Viewing Native American artwork with the intent to
see aesthetic qualities is not a new idea. It has surfaced
several times in the past century, starting in the final decades of the nineteenth century, when the tourism industry
expanded and the Arts and Crafts movement took root in
middle-class American homes. Imported from highly indus-
trialized England, this movement rejected mass-produced

Bowl, c. 1850, artist unknown, Haida; horn, lead(?), 14 × 25 × 12 cm, DAC 300 (cat. no. 185).

objects in favor of handmade goods, and Native American arts—such as California Indian baskets, Mohawk beadwork, and Navajo rugs—fit the bill. While individual objects may not have been considered "art," they were nonetheless displayed as aesthetic objects in their collectors' homes.

One of the earliest scholarly expressions of the kind of aesthetic relativism that would eventually locate Native American objects in the display cases of elite Western art museums was anthropologist Franz Boas's *Primitive Art* (1927), which emphasized that even if an object were not considered "beautiful" to the Western eye, it could still be the product of a valid aesthetic vision. This philosophical position helped viewers see Native American objects as art but relegated the objects to a separate cultural category. Provocative exhibitions in New York City in 1931 (*Exposition of Indian Tribal Art*) and 1941 (*Indian Art of the United States,* at the Museum of Modern Art) supported this view by displaying Indian objects as art, albeit a "primitive" art that required a different mode of perception to be understood and appreciated.

Contemporary Western artists' interest in Native American objects was an important part of this trend. One of these was the American artist Marsden Hartley, whose *Amerika* series of paintings (1914) was inspired by Native American objects in the collection of the Berlin Ethnographic Museum. Such elements as abstracted triangular tipis, striped and circular forms, and stars worked within the artist's expressionist repertoire and rooted his work solidly to his home country while he lived and traveled in Europe. American artists Adolph Gottlieb and Jackson Pollock also found inspiration in Native American culture and motifs.

What these artists saw when they looked at petroglyphs or reproductions of Navajo sand paintings was not artifact, but art: fantastic forms dancing on unconventional canvases and creating bold compositions, dynamic textures, and powerful interplays of light and shadow. This encouraged non-Native collectors and institutions to find artistic value in Native American art, but persistent evolutionary beliefs that Native Americans were not only different but culturally inferior kept it segregated in its own category of the "primitive."

The new value accorded primitive art fueled collectors' desires for what they considered to be "pure," "original," or "authentic" Native American art, the authenticity of an object being measured by its proximity to the baseline of an (imaginary) original, static culture. Desire for "authentic" objects persisted despite the fact that techniques and forms were continually changing, with the consequence that much innovative Native American art was ignored until the advent of multiculturalism.

In the midst of renewed interest in Native American cultural identity in the 1960s and 1970s, multiculturalism put a spotlight on contemporary, mostly formally trained Native American artists and succeeded in catching the attention of some major art-world institutions, such as the Whitney Museum of American Art. But multiculturalism often promoted ethnic segregation, with minority artists grouped together in special shows. Traditional arts and artists enjoyed the expanded marketplace provided since 1922 by the Santa Fe Indian Market and since the 1970s by national auctions, and prices rose. But the general perception of Native American objects as artifacts, or, at best, "primitive" art, did not change.

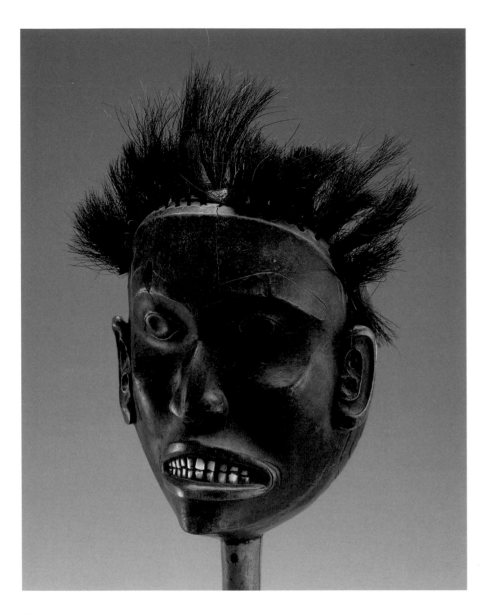

Rattle, c. 1780, artist unknown,
Tsimshian; wood, hair, bone, nails,
pigment, sinew, rattling material,
37 × 20 × 14 cm, DAC 664
(cat. no. 112).

Opposite: **Boy's shirt**, c. 1880,
artist unknown, Crow; hide, wool,
sinew, cotton thread, 59 × 120 ×
3 cm, DAC 415 (cat. no. 101).
Cane, c. 1850, artist unknown,
Woodlands culture; wood, ferrous
screw, ferrous nails, pigment, 92 ×
8 × 8 cm, DAC 189 (cat. no. 91).
Baby carrier, c. 1870, artist
unknown, Kiowa; hide, wood,
cotton fabric, glass beads, copper

alloy (brass), iron, cotton thread,
110 × 34 × 25 cm, DAC 416 (cat.
no. 102). **Sash**, 1780–1800, artist
unknown, Choctaw; wool, glass
beads, cordage, 9 × 144 × .5 cm,
DAC 500 (cat. no. 104). **Moccasins**,
c. 1870, artist unknown, Kiowa;
hide, glass beads, sinew, pigment,
10 × 9 × 48 cm each, DAC 104
(cat. no. 89).

In 1998, the Dikers' own collection was exhibited at the
Metropolitan Museum of Art. In many ways this was a coup:
even though the display cases were relegated to a hallway,
instead of being mounted in a room of their own, a review
in the *New York Times* lauded the aesthetic qualities of the
individual objects. But the exhibition and the accompanying catalogue were divided into regions, which emphasized
cultural differences rather than cross-cultural connections.

With *First American Art*, the NMAI is not rejecting past
approaches but rather building on them to construct a new
paradigm that allows Native American art to engage in a
dialogue with other forms of art. This new paradigm is organized around universal aesthetic concepts—such as idea,
emotion, and vocabulary—that enable us to verbalize what
is good, truthful, or beautiful about any work of art. By any
standard, the exhibition's organizing principles represent a
radical departure from conventional modes of display for
Native American art. To understand the dimensions of this
departure, an overview of the history of the collecting and
interpretating of Native American art is helpful.

The history of collecting Native American art parallels the
history of European Contact and stems from the larger historical phenomenon of Western desire for exotic objects.
The first non-Native American collectors of Native American objects were European explorers, who returned from
the New World in the first centuries of colonialism with
ships filled with so-called natural (flora and fauna) and arti-
ficial (man-made) souvenirs. These souvenirs were installed
in curiosity cabinets—common features of royal and noble
households throughout Europe at the time—that were to
become the foundations of many of Europe's major museums. Objects collected during this initial period of Contact
are considered a baseline for authenticity by collectors
seeking "pure" or "real" Indian objects, despite the fact that
styles and forms had been changing for centuries as a result
of contacts within and among tribes.

Collecting for American museums reached its height
later, in the 1800s. In the wake of westward expansion and
the "pacification" of tribes, early explorers such as Meri-
wether Lewis and William Clark were replaced by ethnolo-
gists, many of whom were hired by the U.S. government to

Olla, c. 1885, artist unknown,
Chemehuevi; willow, Martynia,
33 × 38 cm, DAC 412 (cat. no. 191).

gather the remnants of what it considered to be a vanishing culture. Up to this point, most of the objects being collected had been made for internal use by members of the artist's tribe or for trade to members of another tribe. Many of these objects incorporated non-Native materials, such as beads, or were made with European tools; because they were made for the use of tribal members, however, they provide another important baseline for authenticity against which later objects made for sale to outsiders are measured.

The manufacture of objects for sale to outsiders accelerated dramatically to meet the demands of tourism. Increased demand for Indian products in the early decades of the twentieth century helped revitalize some tribal industries and encouraged the use of innovative materials. This expansion of the market to include items made for sale to outsiders raised the status and price of pre-Contact objects, which by this time were accessible only to museums and wealthy private collectors. The continual displacement of objects from Indian communities to urban homes and museums moved the collecting setting from rural areas to urban galleries and auction houses; it also contributed to the perception of Native American objects as "primitive" art by juxtaposing them with modern European and American artworks, from which they appeared radically different.

In New York City, historical Yup'ik masks that had been deaccessioned from the massive collection of George Gustav Heye (other parts of which later became the core of the collection of the NMAI) were sold by art and antiquities dealers to elite artists such as André Breton and Max Ernst. These artists turned to what they called "primitive" art to inspire them in an age of industrialization and conformity. But the vast distance between the living, named artist and the dead, unnamed "muse" was always maintained. It was the twentieth century, the "Indian wars" were over, and the frontier was closed; with the American government championing progress and assimilation, few collectors felt the need to concern themselves with the provenance of objects.

Because all historical Native American art was collected in the context of colonialism, provenance is not always easy to determine. Historians, anthropologists, and even collectors are quick to acknowledge America's long history of physical and cultural violence toward tribal people, but to incorporate this history into the provenance of an object is a different and difficult undertaking, because it raises the question of why we covet objects that either have been obtained through violence or have become symbolic of the violence of colonialism. Partly in an effort to acknowledge this issue, the Native American Graves Protection and Repatriation Act (NAGPRA, or Public Law 101-601), passed by Congress in 1990, bans trade in funerary objects, sacred objects, and objects of cultural patrimony and requires the repatriation of such objects from federally funded museum collections. Repatriation from private collections, however, is voluntary. In many cases, collectors might not be aware that they own objects that a particular tribe considers sacred; even if they are aware, it is often difficult for them to know how to proceed outside the official infrastructure of a museum or other institution. And because no financial compensation is provided to individuals or institutions for the repatriation of objects, a significant loss can be incurred.

Collecting in the age of repatriation entails paying close attention to the cultural context of objects and being aware of the political circumstances of their provenance. It is an important component of the larger project to acknowledge the sovereignty of and to repair relations with Native American tribes. In an exhibition of this nature, the challenge is to remain aware of these issues while foregrounding the aesthetic qualities of the objects.

It is difficult to regulate our responses—political, emotional, aesthetic, social—to a particular work of art, because those responses will be conditioned by the knowledge and experience we bring to the table. Scholars who have researched the repatriation process extensively might find it difficult to view historical objects without thinking about "battlefield provenance." In studying the Diker collection, however, Native and non-Native curators were quick to point out that many particularly fine objects, such as a pair of beaded children's moccasins, had probably been made for sale to outsiders, or had been sold to outsiders when they were no longer needed. The same curators then turned the conversation toward the aesthetic qualities of the object, commenting on the contrasting colors of the beads, the spare symbolism of the decorative motifs, and the delightful designs beaded onto the sole, which indicated that the shoes had been worn on a special occasion or by an elite wearer.

The political dimensions of collecting historical Native American objects cannot and should not be ignored, but if the goal is to elevate Native-made objects to the status of art, then these dimensions need to be moved to the background. One of the unstated but widely understood requirements for a particular object to be considered art is that it be "timeless," so viewers in any age can appreciate its aesthetic qualities or fine workmanship, regardless of the political or economic networks in which the object was originally (or is currently) engaged. Similarly, for an object to be considered art, its aesthetic quality must be visible—and comprehensible, to some extent—apart from its original cultural context.

But in their eagerness to experience something culturally different, collectors of Native American art often see the cultural qualities of objects above all else. Pots are associated with the earth from which their clay was dug, and this earth becomes something for the collectors to relate to and claim as part of themselves. Stereotypes play a large role in determining the kinds of cultural connections collectors make, as they have played a large role in the writing of Native American history and the marketing of Native American products.

In letting their collecting be guided primarily by aesthetic principles, the Dikers have employed a strategy that moves us closer to seeing Native American objects as art. This is not to say that they don't see the cultural, or the historical, when they examine a finely woven basket or consider adding another Haida frontlet to their collection, but that their intent is to appreciate the aesthetic, both through the acquisition process and by the very personal choices they make when deciding how to display the objects in their home. For in the end it is not just words but the collecting and display of Native American objects in our homes and institutions that tell the marketplace, and the world, where our indigenous arts stand.

If one of their goals was to appreciate Native American objects according to the same aesthetic criteria we use to classify the paintings of Mark Rothko and the sculptures of Louise Nevelson as art, the Dikers had a significant advantage over other collectors of these objects. Before venturing into the realm of Native American objects, Chuck and Valerie collected modern American and European paintings and sculptures as well as pre-Columbian stone and clay figures.

Both Chuck and Valerie are lifelong New Yorkers. Chuck was born and reared in Brooklyn, while Valerie was born and reared in Manhattan. Valerie attended the Dalton School, where she got her first significant exposure to art, then went on to major in dance at Smith College. Chuck attended Harvard College and then went on immediately to Harvard Business School, where he was introduced to Valerie through mutual friends. Valerie married Chuck ten days after her graduation from Smith—"as women were wont

Charles and Valerie Diker's living room, 2003. The Datsolalee basket in the photo at right sits next to the chair at center back. Photograph by Dirk Bakker.

Presentation bowl, 1907, Datsolalee, Washoe; willow, redbud, bracken fern root, 40 × 40 cm, DAC 326 (cat. no. 187).

to do in those days," she smiled—and the two immediately moved back to Manhattan, where Chuck had landed a job as a vice president of marketing at Revlon. Within a year they had their first child.

At Harvard Business School, Chuck had had a roommate who "lived with a lot of art." Instead of decorating his dormitory walls with posters, as many students do, this young man hung "real" paintings that had been sent up to the school by his parents. This piqued Chuck's interest in living with art, and upon his return to New York City he and Valerie started exploring the contemporary art galleries. "We would go on a rainy day, or on weekends," said Valerie. Chuck found that his involvement with the packaging and display of products at Revlon trained his eye, and with Valerie's experience in modern dance, the couple soon discovered they could relate to the vibrant colors and textures of modern art. Looking turned into buying, and buying turned into living with the work with intimacy and passion.

This meant sharing their Mirós and Calders with their three young children, and sometimes also with their children's friends. "When the kids were young," Valerie recalled, "we introduced them to each piece. We told them they were just to look, not to touch." Of course, some of the sculptural works begged to be handled, which Valerie occasionally allowed under her supervision. "We had a Calder sculpture with two parts to it, a 'mobile' on top and a 'stabile' on the bottom. The kids were really interested in that, so we put it

on the living room floor and played with its moving parts. The kids were always very respectful."

As their modern art collection grew, the Dikers were introduced by a friend to pre-Columbian sculpture. "With pop art and op art, contemporary hit a dormant period for us, where everything seemed somewhat derivative. In pre-Columbian art we saw some of the same forms of abstraction [that we had seen and liked in contemporary] and thought there was a certain sophistication to that," said Chuck. With their first purchase of pre-Columbian art, the Dikers entered an entirely new world, one in which, as Chuck saw it, they were "buying the work of a culture, not an artist." Both Chuck and Valerie relished the opportunity to learn about the cultures of pre-Contact Mesoamerica; they even traveled to Guatemala and Mexico to visit Maya sites. Collecting pre-Columbian art worked for them because it was new, it related to their by-now significant collection of large-scale modern paintings and sculptures, and it helped them to see the Western works with new eyes, eyes that had been opened to different forms of abstraction and representation.

Interest in Native American art came a few years later, in 1972, when the Dikers traveled to Santa Fe for what turned out to be the first of many trips to the Southwest. Old friends were going and had invited the Dikers to join them and bring the kids for a family vacation. Unable to resist the local art scene, they ventured into a Taos gallery and discovered Native American baskets. One of these baskets, an Apache olla, became their first purchase of Native American art. The decision to buy the basket surprised them both—they weren't looking to start a new collection, and they hadn't considered baskets to be art. After that experience, Chuck laughed, "We decided baskets were very fine." Like the long faces of pre-Columbian clay figures, the motifs on baskets were "emblematic and abstracted." This made them appealing to the Dikers, who made their visit to Santa Fe an annual tradition. "Within ten minutes of hitting the ground in Santa Fe," Valerie said, "Chuck was in the galleries."

The Dikers continued collecting baskets, displaying them in the home they bought a few years later with their friends in Santa Fe. They took the same approach to Native American that they had to pre-Columbian, seeking out knowledgeable dealers and reading books to learn about the field. To learn what was considered fine, they visited galleries and museums and studied the internal aesthetics of each cultural region. Not surprisingly, baskets were just the beginning; from there, they moved into pottery, then on to Plains and Plateau beadwork.

They started taking pieces back to New York City to display in their apartment, an airy, modern block of rooms occupying the entire seventh floor of a Park Avenue building and overlooking Central Park. "We were surprised when [the Native American art] seemed to fit in so naturally, in such a nonconfrontational way," mused Valerie. "We had read about the concept of juxtaposing modern and primitive art," added Chuck, "and we had been to that show at the Museum of Modern Art." That show, *"Primitivism" in Twentieth-Century Art: Affinity of the Tribal and the Modern*, which exposed New York City to another cycle of the artistic appreciation of indigenous arts, went up in 1984, more than ten years after the Dikers had started collecting Native American art and more than twenty years after they had started collecting modern art. In many ways, the exhibition validated the Dikers' philosophy that tribal art—and Native American art in particular—was worthy of the same level of aesthetic appreciation as modern art.

At the close of the exhibition at the Museum of Modern Art, each piece was gently removed from its case and spirited away to its real home in the collection of American modernist, or cubist, or African art. But in the Dikers' apartment, no such separate collections exist. The Datsolalee

basket (cat. no. 187), serene in its round heft and earthy texture, sits on a small table in front of a Rothko, whose loud blocks of pink, red, and white seem to engulf an entire wall. The room, one of several sitting rooms in the apartment overlooking Central Park, is sparsely furnished, with simple white chairs and couches arranged around glass tables. The entire apartment, in fact, was reconstructed to retain as much unbroken wall space as possible, Chuck explained, to accommodate the many large-scale paintings. The room's other walls are all but entirely covered with large works by Dine, Nevelson, and Reinhardt. Highlighted in one of the windows overlooking the park is one of the Dikers' few contemporary Native American pieces, a detailed doll by prize-winning Luiseño artist Jamie Okuma. Another of Okuma's dolls graces a small table.

One of their few remaining pieces of pre-Columbian work (most of this collection was given away, with a few pieces ending up in the Metropolitan Museum of Art) sits prominently on the center table. Despite its relatively small size, this piece is often the focus of attention for guests, said Valerie. Somehow the large pieces don't overshadow the smaller ones; in fact, they resonate, each providing a fresh view of the other. To see these pieces in juxtaposition with one another—not just in the context of a museum exhibition, but in a room whose contents are lived with every day—is to see them in a new light.

At one point during our visit with the Dikers, J. J. Brody, a specialist on the Southwest, brought a delicate white-washed Ako olla (cat. no. 5) into the dining room and set it on a sideboard, where it was bathed in bright light. Like the sitting rooms, this room was large and sparsely furnished. On its walls hung not one but two immense Jean Dubuffets, a colorful Calder mobile with swinging coils and concentric circles, and a heavy Julian Schnabel collage of broken porcelain plates. The intent of the curator was to deliver an impromptu lecture on the provenance of the pot, whose unidentified maker had decorated it with what the curator suggested are symbolic images and had left small fingerprints on the unglazed inside lip. But seeing the pot there, lit by a spotlight and dwarfed by the more sculptural of the two Dubuffets, one could not help but think of the pot as sculpture and rhythm, and of the Dubuffet as essential and organic. It was a dialogue that was hard to articulate but impossible to escape; nor was it merely a dialogue but a conversation in which each piece's truths were mediated and filtered through a third party, the viewer. Ideally, the dialogue wouldn't privilege any one aesthetic system, so that composition wouldn't supersede symbolic repetition or balance and each piece could be "read" from the point of view of the other. After listening to Brody's presentation, we were all better informed about the daily lives of Acoma women and the function of pottery in the village. Our attention turned to the next item, an elaborately embroidered Ojibwe bag, but the unspoken dialogue remained, a near-silent hum waiting to be given breath.

The visual dialogue between modern artworks is commonly spoken and written about, not just by critics but also by the artists themselves. This is one of the great pleasures of collecting modern art: being able to hear, and sometimes even participate in, the intellectual process of interpretation. And it marks one of the most significant differences between collecting modern European and American art and historical Native American art, since most of the latter has not been or cannot be attributed to a particular artist and is most frequently interpreted from a great historical distance by non-Native critics. This difference

doesn't bother the Dikers, who—unlike many other collectors of Native American art—aren't looking to become part of a Native community or to develop relationships with the artists. When they owned a home in Santa Fe, the Dikers attended Pueblo feast days and the open houses of Valerie's favorite contemporary jewelers, Denise Wallace and the team of Gail Bird and Yazzie Johnson. They still regularly attend Indian Market and make purchases of contemporary jewelry and beadwork; they also contribute their time and money to Native organizations and organizations that support Native causes. But their primary relationships are not with the artists, but the objects.

And with each other. "It's a very important thing to have a common interest in a marriage," said Chuck. They both love collecting art and living with it in their home. "Art is like children; it's a second thing to share," said Chuck. They don't buy anything that they don't both like, and they sometimes test their synchronicity by visiting galleries independently and each picking out a favorite piece. More often than not, they discover later, their picks are the same.

The Dikers make no apologies for not collecting contemporary Native American art, aside from dolls and jewelry. From what they can see, much contemporary Native

Hat, c. 1820, artist unknown, Maliseet; cloth, glass beads, 17 × 17.5 cm, DAC 724 (cat. no. 25).

American art—by which they mean the ubiquitous pots, baskets, and katsinas that are sold throughout the Southwest—is derivative. "What doesn't interest us," Valerie explained, "is contemporary artists who try to re-create the old." Innovation, however, is something they support, but in the genre of contemporary Native American art, they have only recently been exposed to it. Besides the dolls and the jewelry, the only piece of contemporary Native American art displayed in their apartment is a blown and sandblasted glass bowl, which they purchased directly from the artist, Preston Singletary, after losing a similar piece to the Pequot Tribe at an auction. Because their wall space is nearly entirely covered with modern paintings, they also cannot consider adding any "flat art" to their collection, be it a historical Navajo blanket or a new painting by Harry Fonseca, who was invited to help design the exhibition and who participated in the meeting at the Dikers' apartment. "We will not collect for storage!" exclaimed Valerie.

Nor do the Dikers harbor any illusion that their collecting of historical material "helps" Native people in any way. Rather than purchase items they do not like from living artists, the Dikers choose to provide support in a more general way by making donations to Native American nonprofit organizations such as the Southwest-based Wings for America and Futures for Children.

With their knowledge base, economic resources, and collecting prowess, the Dikers have been invited to serve on the boards of several museums. They have served on the board of directors of the NMAI since it opened, and have also served on the board of the Museum of New Mexico and on the acquisition committee of the Whitney. Their relationships with institutions put them in a unique position to expose not only their collection but also their philosophies to a wide audience. By displaying their collection at the Metropolitan—an institution accustomed to displaying objects as "art" but one that rarely presents Native American objects—the Dikers hoped to reach a new audience and to impress upon that audience that Native American objects could and should be included in the museum's collection. When the NMAI approached the Dikers about exhibiting their by-now expanded collection a few years later, Chuck recognized an opportunity to accomplish the same goal in a different way. "The NMAI is a good counterpoint to the Met," Chuck said, "because of its different location and audience." While visitors to the NMAI are accustomed to seeing Native American objects, they may not be accustomed to seeing these objects displayed as art. "[In the past] Native American art has been shown—especially at the museum on 155th Street [where the Heye collection was previously exhibited]—in darkness and in overcrowded cases. It's the same at the [American] Museum of Natural History, where [objects are] thrown together like a bunch of crafts from another time." It's not a matter of respect, Chuck suggested, but a matter of approach: "the objects are just not presented in a way that maximizes their aesthetic beauty."

Although we cannot anticipate the success of this exhibition in changing the perception of Native American art in the long term, we can hope that the Dikers' approach to collecting will strike a chord with viewers and that a renewed appreciation of aesthetics will guide the collecting and display of Native American art in the twenty-first century.

Kiowa Chief

DONALD KUSPIT

The Spiritual

IMPORT OF NATIVE AMERICAN AESTHETICS

The mana *of the Polynesians, the* manitou *of the Algonquin tribes, the* orenda *of the Iroquois, etc. have as their common factor the concept and intuition of an increased efficacy as such, transcending all mere "natural" bonds; no sharp distinction is made between the particular potencies of this efficacy, between its modes and forms. Mana is attributed equally to mere things and to persons, to "spiritual" and "material," to "animate" and "inanimate" entities.*

—Ernst Cassirer, *The Philosophy of Symbolic Forms*, vol. 2, *Mythical Thought*[1]

It will not, then, surprise us to find that it is not only in connection with natural objects (such as the dewdrop) or events (such as death) but also in connection with works of art, and in fact whenever or wherever perception (aesthesis) leads to a serious experience, that we are really shaken.

—Ananda Coomaraswamy, "Samvega: Aesthetic Shock"[2]

Yet the contents and structures of the unconscious are the result of immemorial existential situations, especially of critical situations, and this is why the unconscious has a religious aura. For every existential crisis once again puts in question both the reality of the world and man's presence in the world. This means that the existential crisis is, finally, "religious," since on the archaic levels of culture being and the sacred are one.

—Mircea Eliade, *The Sacred and the Profane*[3]

LET'S TAKE THE BULL BY THE HORNS: I WANT TO DE-EMPHASIZE THE CULTURAL, emphasize the aesthetic aspect—the sensuous elegance and power, which invariably signify spiritual depth and complexity[4]—of Native American art. Not that the cultural factor isn't there, but that, in my understanding, culture is an expressive filter for spiritual consciousness, not the other way round. Spiritual consciousness is not culturally determined, nor is it a naive subjective epiphenomenon of socially real experience. Perhaps the cultural reification of spiritual consciousness can catalyze it, but then only under certain hypnotic ceremonial conditions—social conditions meant to control its participants—which may be a mechanical yea-saying of spirituality rather than an authentic initiation into it.[5] That is, the system of

Opposite: ***Twelve High-Ranking Kiowa Men*** (detail), c. 1880, Julian Scott Ledger Artist B, Kiowa; paper, ink, colored pencil, 18.5 × 31 cm, DAC 059LD (cat. no. 88).

ritual is an administered act of social obedience with little resemblance to the spontaneous surge of awe that testifies to the presence of the living spirit, and with that to the radical self-transformation called a conversion experience. A spiritual ceremony is supposed to be an emotional as well as social discipline—an individuating experience as well as a collective event—but it may deceive its practitioners: instead of leading them to self-transcending awareness, it may express their submission to the collective will. Ritual may reify the self into a social thing rather than renew the archaic sense of self in which spirituality is rooted.[6]

Every attempt to rationalize what is transrational—to conventionalize, stabilize, and banalize what is existential, unstable, and numinous, as though it could be mastered by human beings (rather than master them)—sooner or later fails. The spiritual eventually erupts from behind its sociocultural mask—forces its way out of the ill-fitting procrustean bed in which society restrains it—shocking one into awareness of its power. Spiritual consciousness may engage features of the natural and social environment, incorporating them in its visions, but it uses them to symbolize what transcends every particular environment—mana, manitou, orenda, to refer to the Cassirer epigraph—and as such is sacred, that is, an enigmatic efficacy. It cannot be reduced to the literal environment ("region") in which it occurs, but rather informs that environment so that it seems spiritually significant—a sacred space.

As Eliade writes, consciousness of the sacred becomes manifest in the "paradigmatic manner" of mythical image,[7] and a mythical consciousness of the sacred efficacy that makes existence possible and sanctifies it—reveals it to be sacred outwardly and inwardly, in appearance as well as reality, in feeling as well as fact—is part of what Native American art is about, whatever else it is about. If, as Cassirer writes, what distinguishes the revelations of perception and intuition from the representations of conceptual knowledge is that "they are supposed at least to stand in direct contact" with what they reveal, then Native American art is an archaic art of revelation—like all so-called primitive art—however much it makes use of what Cassirer calls "representative signs."[8] Its signs epitomize the sacred—thus their "magical" efficacy—rather than routinely signify it. They establish contact with it, and as such are a form of concrete

thinking. They do not simply represent it, so that it seems to "recede into the distance," as Cassirer says,[9] but rather invite "mystical participation" in the sacred, as Coomaraswamy says.[10] It is only through the mythical image—not through the conceptualized sign—that such a merger with the sacred can occur, bringing with it the realization of the sacredness of one's own existence and all existence (which is what Native American creation myths celebrate).[11] In short, much of Native American art is essentially a sacred—which means existentially primary—art, whatever its secular use and cultural implications. It is eagerly collected not because it has become a prized luxury good, but because of the mana-manitou-orenda latent in it, which spontaneously moves people—"shakes" them to the bottom of their being, as Coomaraswamy says—whatever their culture and society. It is indeed a luxury, but an expressive luxury, for it affords an aesthetic shock of existential recognition. It conveys a spiritual attitude to life increasingly rare in our secular society.

In fact, when Janet Berlo and Ruth Phillips write that "the sacred/secular dichotomy is [a] Western overlay on Native modes of thinking,"[12] and that "phrases in Plains languages reveal that people adorned themselves 'in proper relationship to the gods,'" and that "in some cases, powerful items of ceremonial gear were described in words whose approximate translation is 'something sacred wears me,' a reversal of ordinary assumptions about who is the wearer and what is worn,"[13] they are acknowledging the primacy of spiritual experience—the pervasiveness of the sense of the sacred—in the most intimate details of Native American life. When Jackson Pollock and other American artists professed interest in Native American art, whatever their vague understanding of it, they were acknowledging, with a kind of innocent awe, its spiritual character. Its elaborate geometry, auratic colors, and intense figuration—it is invariably dignified and self-contained, however sometimes forbidding and monstrous—are an aesthetic triumph of spiritual expression. Whatever the collective character and import of Native American art objects, they are individualized expressions of the universal efficacy—be it called mana, manitou, orenda, or wakanda (Sioux)—that transcends collective identity.

What are the main aesthetic features of these objects? The Diker collection suggests that there are two broad

Pipe, c. 1780, artist unknown, Eastern Woodlands; wood, metal (lead?), ferrous nails(?), 9.5 × 18 × 8 cm, DAC 531 (cat. no. 133).

categories of Native American art: pure abstractions and figural abstractions, whether the figure be a plant, an animal, or a human being. The figure is generally schematic, losing its roundedness, which makes it emblematic without losing its vitality. That is, however abstract, the figure seems vibrantly alive—inwardly animated. The spirit dwells in it, making it seem transnatural as well as natural. (Examples include cat. nos. 13, 14, 28, 29, 37, 50, 99, 123, 126, 127, 141, 146, 147, 150, 153, 157, 168, 173, 184.) The pure abstraction tends to be an ornamental pattern—a dynamic sacred design, sanctifying the everyday object (moccasin, basket, jar, etc.) it adorns. (Examples include cat. nos. 1, 6, 32, 36, 38, 40, 60–63, 67–70, 89, 94, 95, 97, 124, 125, 128, 130, 145, 150, 152, 154, 155, 156, 158, 163, 177, 182, 188, 191, 194, 196.)

Just as cave paintings are informed by the irregular stone walls on which they are inscribed—the animal body is often built around an outcropping of rock—so Native American patterns are an intimate dimension of the objects (soft or hard) they "bless," rather than superimposed on them as an extraneous sign or arbitrary marker. In other words, the objects are not simply a kind of blank canvas that the patterned image or imagistic design fills and hides, however much, in modern art, some of the blankness may be used as negative pictorial space—the space of absence reinforcing the presence of the primary representation—but rather are integrated with the artistic image, often to the extent of for-

mally echoing it as well as being materially one with it. Also, in both cases, closed figure—whether mandala-like pattern or seemingly archetypal presence—and open ground are usually flat surfaces, as though acknowledging the basic surface of the object. Indeed, however much the figure seems to finesse the surface by dramatically standing out from it, the figure remains grounded in the surface and thus "part" of the object—essential to its identity, in whatever obscure way. Even when the image depicts an obviously round object, it is usually flattened into planarity, as seen in cat. no. 4, where a gourd is spread out like an animal hide. It is in effect shown in its totality in both profile and full-face, as it were, like a faceted cubist figure.

And even when the surface is raised in quasi-relief, as occurs when it is made of beads or porcupine quills or some other collaged material arranged with mosaic-like meticulousness, it is experienced as a flat space (even an infinite plane), and as such an inner space, that is, a space in which representations are by definition spiritual, if only because they are displaced from the roundedness of external reality. Are the additive feathers that often form a kind of material aura around certain objects displaced roundedness? I think so, just as the pure patterns, which often have a centralized design, use the center to suggest projection. The design is often repetitively spread over the surface of the object, creating an all-over effect that serves to make the object more emphatically present even while suggesting that it is a materialization of spirit. Background object and foreground design or figure become undifferentiated spirit-matter. Thus, like Native American three-dimensional figures and masks, the object becomes what Robert Plant Armstrong calls a profoundly "affecting presence."[14]

Now it seems to me that a fundamental way of understanding the expressive complexity of Native American art objects is through Wilhelm Worringer's distinction between abstraction and empathy. "Whereas the precondition for the urge to empathy is a happy pantheistic relationship of confidence between man and the phenomena of the external world," Worringer writes, "the urge to abstraction is the outcome of a great inner unrest inspired in man by the phenomena of the outside world; in a religious respect it corresponds to a strongly transcendental tinge to all notions. We might describe this state as an immense spiritual dread

Bag (details), c. 1820, artist unknown, Great Lakes; vegetal fiber (hemp?), wool, 14 × 20.3 cm, DAC 672 (cat. no. 52).

of space."[15] That dreadful space is especially evident in Native American narrative images—communal scenes and scenes of warfare—where the figures barely hold their own against the space. They seem superficial compared to its expanse—not simply the expanse of the plains, or of nature in general, but the expanse of infinity. They survive in it only as abstractions—as transcendental imagistic notions, as it were.

However active in this cosmic environment, human beings are never anchored in it. They are radically apart—altogether different, incommensurate dimensions of being. Human existence is not innate to it, but passes through it. In these narrative scenes the figures are like so many footprints in the desert, traces of a humanity that has no effect on it. It is as though the empty space has drained them of organic richness. It has been displaced onto their ornament, which is nonetheless as paradigmatic and abstract as they are. The space is often crowded with figures—some of the works suggest a *horror vacui*, an appropriate response to the threat of annihilation the space unconsciously represents—but the figures, often with accompanying horses and houses, are weightless (there is no sense of solid earth and the pull of gravity), making the event illustrated—usually an occurrence in which the existence of the community is at risk—seem imaginary. The scenes have an innocent hallucinatory quality, suggesting that they are a dream version of history. They are not an accurate record but an event revisited in a trancelike state that mythologizes it into a collective memory. These Native American narrative works have the look of medieval imagery in both the static insularity of their figures—however dynamic in themselves—and in their transcendental space.

But the majority of the Native American art objects do something different: they brilliantly integrate pantheistic empathy, which involves, as Worringer writes, "the reproduction of organically beautiful vitality,"[16] and transcendental abstraction, which involves "taking the individual thing of the external world out of its arbitrariness and seeming fortuitousness, . . . eternalising it by approximation to abstract forms and, in this manner, . . . finding a point of tranquility and a refuge from appearances."[17] Pure pattern is the ultimate refuge from external appearances, but the bright colors and intricate design of the pattern distill the excitement of organically beautiful vitality. The pattern is not entirely purified of "its dependence upon life," however much it asserts "*absolute* value."[18] It is a "pure geometric abstraction," but the "caprice of perception" remains an indispensable, vitalizing part of it.[19] The Native American art object is a masterful aesthetic synthesis of repose and restlessness, so much so that it is difficult to decide or tell which is immanent, which transcendent.

For Worringer, ornament is "the fundament of all aesthetic consideration of art." "The artistic volition of a people finds its purest and most unobscured expression" in ornament. "Figurative art is one-sidedly preferred as the so-called higher art . . . [although it tells us less] . . . about the aesthetic endowment of a people . . . [than] its ornament."[20] The point is decisively hammered home in Markus Brüderlin's demonstration of "ornament's [profound] influence on the genesis and development of abstract art."[21] Basing himself on Worringer's ideas, as well as Alois Riegl's call "for the recognition of the purely artistic essence of the ornament independent of function, technique and material," thus "free[ing] ornament from its inferior status as decoration and establish[ing] it as an independent formal category," Brüderlin argues that seemingly autonomous abstraction is in effect "a continuation of the history of ornament."[22] Brüderlin's ideas, and those developed by his colleagues, who trace the dependence of modern abstraction on primitive ornament—in rebuttal of Adolf Loos's 1898 polemical view that "the less advanced a nation, the more extravagant its ornaments, its decoration, . . . taking the Indians . . . as [one] example"[23]—make it clear that Native American ornamental abstraction is a major current in the mainstream of archaicizing abstraction. It is among the clearest examples of the "elementary urge to decorate," as Riegl put it. He regarded it as an expression of "free creative will," arguing that "richly decorating all functional objects but also the body" is a "purely creative activity."[24] What he neglects to say is that such pure creative activity is an expression of spiritual consciousness, which is a dialectic of empathic delight in the "euphony" of natural rhythms and the pursuit of an abstract "perfection" that seems to transcend nature even as it informs it (these are Worringer's terms). This dialectic is magnificently evident in many Native American art objects, three-dimensional as well as two-dimensional, for example, in the two-dimensional objects shown in cat. nos. 168 and 173, and the three-dimensional ones in cat. nos. 44 and 132. Indeed, abstraction is used to transform a functional object—including the naturally given objects on which Native American existence depended—into an affective presence, in effect giving it a new spiritual identity,

or rather bringing out its inherently spiritual character. Even animals and plants are capable of having spiritual consciousness—indeed, of embodying it rather than merely symbolizing it—for the Native American artists who made these objects.

Perhaps the most salient examples of the reconciliation of empathy and abstraction in Native American art are the explicitly cosmological images. Human figures and animals are arranged systematically around an abstract center emblematic of the universe. Cat. nos. 37 and 99, both Apache trays, are superb examples. The center is circular, however faceted the circle sometimes is—each facet suggests an aspect of the cosmic order, but all facets are connected and integrated into that order, that is, they form a cosmic whole and the object itself is circular. Thus microcosmic center and macrocosmic object are united through the intermediate band of human and animal figures—the human and natural orders, which have a certain parity, as the placement of human beings and animal next to each other in an alternating pattern suggests. All have the same abstract, paradigmatic, archaic character, and all are enclosed within the perimeter of the object—hermetically sealed, as the thick outline of the edge suggests—confirming their unity in a sacred cosmic order. Human beings,

Tray, c. 1880, artist unknown, Western Apache; willow, Martynia, cottonwood, 10 × 32 cm, DAC 381 (cat. no. 37).

animals, even plant life are all in carefully equilibrated relationship to each. One has the sense of a harmonious universe in which everything has its particular place, even as it exists anonymously in cosmic space. As Eliade says, "this conscious repetition of given paradigmatic gestures reveals an original ontology. . . . The gesture acquires meaning, reality, solely to the extent to which it repeats a primordial act."[25] The figures are transient gestures in the eternal cosmos, acquiring meaning only by being repeated and linked together, and, perhaps above all, being similar. Is it the case that only through their art objects could Native Americans express their difference and individuality, which otherwise would threaten the community's need to hold together—to form a unified if hierarchical collective whole—in order to survive in the cosmic environment they inhabited?

I submit that, precisely by placing themselves in the cosmic scheme of things, Native Americans deny the precariousness of an existence directly dependent on nature while implicitly acknowledging that precariousness by showing themselves "abandoned" in infinite space. They may be linked together in a community—in cat. no. 37 they hold hands, as though in a ceremonial dance (the figures are marked by crosses, suggesting the integration of Christianity into archaic ritual—it has its own archaic rituals)—but the community exists in a cosmic void. The figures can disappear into it at any moment, as their shadowy character—they are more phantom than solid, let

alone durable, substance—suggests. "Settling in a territory is equivalent to founding a world," Eliade writes,[26] and "the true world is always . . . at the Center, for it is here that there is a break in plane and hence communication among the three cosmic zones."[27] Thus "the religious man sought to live as near as possible to the Center of the World,"[28] and "feels the need always to exist in a total and organized world, in a cosmos."[29] "It follows that every construction or fabrication has the cosmogony as paradigmatic model"[30]—including every Native American functional/art object.

But Eliade neglects to note that such cosmogonic constructions, with their centralized character and all-encompassing order, are security systems. More particularly, they represent what Harry Stack Sullivan calls "the self-system for the avoiding or minimizing of anxiety or for the concealing of anxiety, the self-system [which] has . . . some aspects which can be said to be . . . directed to keep one safe from any possibility of passing into that extremely unpleasant state of living which can be called the uncanny emotions."[31] These become explicit in situations of disaster but are always latent. The cosmographic constructions are in effect emblems of these artists' Native American selves—the strong, ordered, carefully centered ego they needed to survive in raw nature, which for all its cyclic character has a certain capriciousness that threatened community disaster. Perhaps above all, the uncanny, seeming limitless space the artists inhabited—a space of open horizons, mountains

Moccasins, c. 1875, artist unknown, Kiowa; hide, glass beads, tinned iron, wool, pigment, cotton thread, 9 × 10 × 43 cm each, DAC 281 (cat. no. 97).

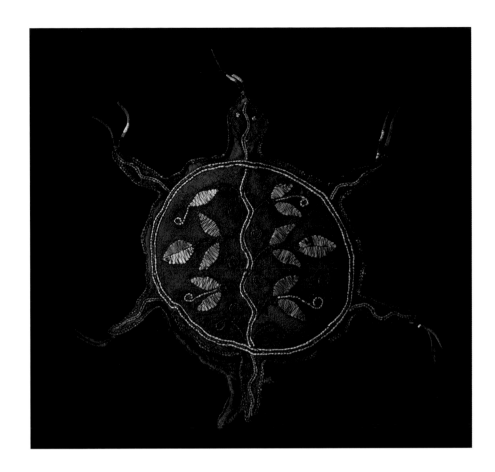

Bag, c. 1800, artist unknown,
Eastern Great Lakes; hide,
porcupine quill, cotton(?)
thread, 26.7 × 24.1 cm,
DAC 715 (cat. no. 58).

that had no human measure, and dangerous animals—was anxiety-arousing, however unconsciously. Inhabiting an orderly cosmos, they felt safe and secure, however aware they were of its uncanny nature, on which they were totally dependent. Embedded in its material place in the cosmos, like the animal and the human figure in cat. no. 52—who seems to have a snake in each hand, as though performing a ritual—every being could feel secure in itself and in relation to every other being. Knowing one's place in the cosmos seems crucial to these artists, if only because it generated a sense of safety.

What then is one to make of such eccentric—certainly disruptive—designs as the pattern that appears on the object in cat. no. 186? It seems a long way from the rhythmic coherence of those in cat. nos. 36 and 187. More generally, what is one to make of the abrupt change in pattern that occurs in many of the objects, for example, that in cat. no. 137, with its juxtaposition of a pure geometrical order with a system of repeating leaves (united by the use of the same primary colors, blue and red), or in cat. no. 141, with its juxtaposition of a centralized floral pattern and alternating vertical bands? I submit that they articulate the anxiety—the uncanny sense of coming-apartness of cosmos and, with it, self—that is repressed in the more obviously

ordered cosmographic designs. In my opinion it is the same threatening sense of disintegration—physical as well as psychic annihilation—that is represented by the supernatural animal monsters that inhabit Native American myths. One makes an appearance in cat. no. 190. They are denizens of the emotional depths whatever their resemblance to actual animals. The merger of animal and human seen in cat. no. 44 suggests as much.

The ordered cosmographic pattern is an apotropaic device—something used to ward off disaster and death. The placement of such a pattern on the hide of a dead animal—see cat. no. 10—makes the point succinctly. The wilderness is conquered, but these Native American artists remained attuned to it—necessarily so, because disregard of it can lead to death. Catastrophic death is in fact its secret. I suggest that what makes Native American art objects seem so alive is that they convey mastery of the anxiety induced by the uncanniness of primordial nature—Nathaniel Hawthorne marvelously conveys it in his stories of its effect on early Euro-American society—even as the tensions in their abstract patterns imply it. Whether they radiate joie de vivre or terror, their optical intensity and textural intimacy has something uncanny about it, which is what makes them emotionally profound as well as physically elegant.

Notes

1. Ernst Cassirer, *The Philosophy of Symbolic Forms,* vol. 2, *Mythical Thought,* trans. Ralph Manheim (New Haven and London: Yale University Press, 1955), 158–59.

2. Ananda K. Coomaraswamy, "Samvega: Aesthetic Shock," in *Selected Papers,* vol. 1, *Traditional Art and Symbolism* (Princeton: Princeton University Press, 1977), 182.

3. Mircea Eliade, *The Sacred and the Profane: The Nature of Religion* (New York and Evanston: Harper and Row, 1961), 210.

4. Here I disagree with Coomaraswamy. For me, the aesthetic and the sacred are inseparable rather than at odds. Coomaraswamy, celebrating primitive mentality at the expense of Western mentality—a fashionable way of moving the marginal to the center as well as a trendy turning of a conventional hierarchy upside down, so that what was once devalued and underprivileged becomes the unconventional, overprivileged, highest value—writes: "The purpose of primitive art, being entirely different from the aesthetic or decorative intentions of the modern 'artist' (for whom the ancient motifs survive only as meaningless 'art forms'), explains its abstract character." Coomaraswamy agrees with Lucien Lévy-Bruhl that the purpose of primitive symbols is "not . . . to 'represent' their prototype to the eye, but to facilitate a [mystical] participation," and with Waldemar Deonna that "We civilized men have lost the Paradise of the 'Soul of primitive imagery (*Urbilde*).' We no longer live among the shapes we had fashioned within: we have become mere spectators, reflecting them from without"; see Coomaraswamy, "Primitive Mentality," in *Selected Papers* (note 2), 296. Coomaraswamy thinks that for the modern Western artist "the aesthetic surfaces of phenomena" have no "implications," so that one experiences them as meaningless physical sensations; see "Samvega: Aesthetic Shock," 183.

This dichotomization—the separation of aesthetic surface from spiritual depth (more broadly, sensation from human meaning)—is an intellectualizing error, as Cassirer suggests when he remarks that "myth is originally rooted and . . . forever draws new nourishment" from "*perceptive experience,*" that is, aesthetic experience of phenomena. "Without such a grounding in an original mode of perception, myth would hover in the void; instead of being a universal form of spiritual manifestation, it would be a kind of spiritual disease; however widely distributed, it would still be an accidental and pathological phenomenon"; see *The Philosophy of Symbolic Forms,* vol. 3, *The Phenomenology of Knowledge,* trans. Ralph Manheim (New Haven and London: Yale University Press, 1957), 62. Thus, aesthetic expression is in spontaneous dialectical intimacy with spiritual experience, giving it mythopoetic form while replenishing it. Coomaraswamy is mourning the loss of a primary unity, symbolized by the sacred, but the way to recover this unity is not by regression to the "primitive" but through a new integration of spiritual experience and aesthetic expression. This in fact occurred in nineteenth-century sensuous painting, which in the twentieth century became the pursuit of pure painting—optically pure yet haptically intimate—until it dead-ended in the spiritually empty empirical purity of post-painterly abstraction.

5. I use "spirituality" in the German sense of "Geist," as in Georg Wilhelm Friedrich Hegel's *Phänomenologie des Geistes* and Wassily Kandinsky's *Über das Geistige in der Kunst.* The English word does not resonate with the idea of consciousness the way the German does.

6. I use "archaic" in the basic etymological sense, that is, with reference to "arche" (prototype, original).

7. Eliade, *The Sacred and the Profane* (note 3), 210. Cassirer's account of myth has a certain resemblance to Eliade's. "The farther back we trace perception," Cassirer writes in *The Phenomenology of Knowledge* (note 4), ". . . the more plainly the purely expressive character takes precedence over the matter or thing-character. The understanding of expression is essentially earlier than the knowledge of things." (63) "Myth," he adds, ". . . places us in the living center of this sphere [of expression], for its particularity consists precisely in showing us a mode of world formation which is independent of all modes of mere objectification. It does not recognize the dividing line between real and unreal, between reality and appearance, which theoretical objectivization draws and must draw. . . . The mythical consciousness does not deduce essence from appearance, it possesses—it has—the essence in the appearance. The essence does not recede behind the appearance but is manifested in it; it does not cloak itself in the appearance but in the appearance is given to itself. . . . Thus in the world of myth every phenomenon is always and essentially an incarnation. . . . [T]he world of mythical experience is grounded in experiences of pure expression. . . . What perhaps divides it most sharply from the world of purely theoretical consciousness is the peculiar indifference of the mythical consciousness toward the distinctions of signification and value to which the theoretical consciousness attaches the greatest importance." (67–68) It is worth noting that the aestheticism Coomaraswamy deplores is as far from theoretical consciousness as mythical consciousness, for it not only eschews signification but accords spiritual value to pure sensuousness, in effect mythologizing it.

I use "primitive" here in the sense of a "return to origins." This is the way Cassirer uses it, and Campbell—they also use "mythological" to refer to a mode of thinking or consciousness (which is the way I use it)—and the way Jacques Derrida describes it in *Archive Fever: A Freudian Impression.* It is an accurate usage, despite its association with so-called primitive peoples.

8. Cassirer, *The Phenomenology of Knowledge* (note 4), 47.

9. Ibid., 113.

10. Coomaraswamy, "Primitive Mentality" (note 4), 295.

11. Like Cassirer and Campbell, I use "mythical" to refer to a mode of thinking or consciousness.

12. Janet C. Berlo and Ruth B. Phillips, *Native North American Art* (Oxford and New York: Oxford University Press, 1998), 13.

13. Ibid., 113.

14. In *The Affecting Presence: An Essay in Humanistic Anthropology* (Urbana, Chicago, and London: University of Illinois Press, 1971), Robert Plant Armstrong writes: "The affecting presence

acts as subject, asserting its own being, inviting the perceptor's recognition and, in culturally permitted ways, structuring the subsequent relationship which someone has called 'transaction' in recognition of the fact that while the presence informs the man, the man, in his unique way, to some extent and in some fashion informs the presence. But although the presence is a subject, it is a limited subject. Its limitations are described by its restrictedness, by the extent, indeed, to which it is at the same time an object. It obviously cannot perceive the perceptor; it can only be perceived, owned, created, and disposed of. It is not uncommon, however, to find that its sense of being is so acknowledged that the affecting presence is accorded special treatment—sometimes it receives the attentions and services accorded a person." (25) In Native American society the affecting presence is in fact often part of the person with which it is associated—the spiritual part of the person. Thus moccasins and other items of clothing give the otherwise profane part of the body they cover a spiritual identity, or rather function as an emanation of its inner spirit. Their affecting presence brings it to consciousness of its otherwise unconscious spirituality. The mask is perhaps the most conspicuous example of this.

15. Wilhelm Worringer, *Abstraction and Empathy: A Contribution to the Psychology of Style,* trans. Michael Bullock (New York: International Universities Press, 1953), 15.

16. Ibid., 14.

17. Ibid., 16.

18. Ibid., 17.

19. Ibid., 35.

20. Ibid., 51.

21. Markus Brüderlin, "Introduction: Abstraction and Ornament," in *Ornament and Abstraction: The Dialogue between Non-Western, Modern, and Contemporary Art* (Basel/Riehen: Beyeler Foundation, 2001), 18.

22. Ibid., 18, 21.

23. Dieter Bogner, "The Constructive Ornament—Vienna's Contribution to Abstraction," in *Ornament and Abstraction* (note 21), 36.

24. Ibid.

25. Mircea Eliade, *Cosmos and History: The Myth of the Eternal Return* (New York: Harper and Row, 1954), 5.

26. Eliade, *The Sacred and the Profane* (note 3), 47.

27. Ibid., 42.

28. Ibid., 43.

29. Ibid., 44.

30. Ibid., 45.

31. Harry Stack Sullivan, *The Interpersonal Theory of Psychiatry* (New York: Norton, 1953), 316.

BRUCE BERNSTEIN AND GERALD MCMASTER

The Aesthetic
IN AMERICAN INDIAN ART

> *Like picture writing on utilitarian objects, basketry, pottery, clothing, or in wampum belts or pictographs, these objects as metaphors are not transcriptions of word for word linear sentences but of concepts and processes.*
>
> —Deborah Doxtator (Mohawk)[1]

> *Native American languages are very verb oriented. Similarly, in art it's the process that is really important. For instance, in the making of a mask, the "making" is basically a ritual in itself.*
>
> —Tom Hill (Seneca)[2]

THE TERM "ART" IS NONEXISTENT IN MANY IF NOT ALL AMERICAN INDIAN LANGUAGES. The isolation of ideas into specific definitions as abstract as that of "art" was never a practice among American Indians. Western notions of truth, beauty, and justice did not find equal articulation in most (if any) American Indian cultures, whose philosophical foundations are vastly different from those of the West. Most American Indian cultures and identities are based on the idea of land, a concept far greater and more complex than the word "land" implies to non-Native people. It encompasses not only the land beneath, but the sky above and beyond—in other words, the entire universe of what is both within and without it, the seen and unseen. It is not just a material expression, but also one of origins. Land and Native peoples are inexplicably bound, the creation of people and their arts intertwined with the making of the Earth. Expressions of the idea of *land* vary greatly among the many American Indian cultures, however, because they live in a vast variety of environments and speak hundreds of different languages. It may be less problematic to propose instead the possibility of an American Indian aesthetic to replace the notion of universal art.

To begin, let us assume that every culture has an aesthetic system, a way of looking at and representing the world that influences the way artists express themselves in relation to the surrounding world. All cultures create objects for different reasons and purposes: religious, spiritual, and practical. Regardless, as the object is created, it is imbued with the full measure of its culture and context: philosophy, language, environment, and time. Artists need only to develop their skills at creating objects, since they are already born into and understand the discursive frameworks of their cultures. Equally understood are existing limitations. Nonetheless there always are artists who introduce new perspectives—new ways of creating the

Opposite: ***Powder horn*** (detail), c. 1812, artist unknown, Iroquois; horn (bovine), 30 × 8 cm, DAC 555 (cat. no. 11).

object—by breaking new ground through the introduction of new materials or ideas.

Individuals are not slaves to their culture—otherwise we would all be spiritless instruments. Each of us participates in the collective celebration of culture as a basis for community identity, whether it is through family, beliefs, rituals, ceremonies, war, or other means. Within a culture, however, individuals or groups can operate within more narrowly defined identities. That is, individuals may cross many discursive boundaries, passing through many of life's phases, experiencing the world in different ways, operating within different mental capacities, and having various opinions and convictions. How the individual constructs these webs of meanings within a culture, for whatever reason, creates individuality. It is this individuality that is paramount as we view and think about the works in this exhibition, for it is the individual who has seen the world in new ways from within the larger cultural perspective. These works may vary either slightly or radically from a culturally defined aesthetic structure, but in all we find a complex set of ideas that have been individually articulated. The artist stands out as a keen and articulate observer of culture and its existing traditions, as well as of its multiple influences, materials, techniques, and ideas. Artists make culture material, creating forms that can be worn, handled, or experienced by all people—whether they know the artist or are family or tribal members. Their work integrates ideas from the outside world in ways that are often seamless. While what we see and how we see are closely tied to the ways we are encouraged, allowed, and taught to see, the artist's power of personal expression and individual identity and voice remain important.[3]

Another assumption made here is that the meanings of a work of art converge in significant, unexpected, and discoverable ways, where the work is assumed to be a discrete object with its own internal or essential meanings. Although that work of art is produced within a cultural system, it is much more than a social document transparently mirroring life. The American Indian aesthetic generally has a moral basis, as revealed by the fact that in many Native languages the same word means "beautiful" and "good." Thus, American Indian works of art should be both beautiful and good because they are intended to please the eye as well as the spirits by upholding moral values. Moreover, beauty lies in more than just what we see; it derives its meaning from a collective sense of societal responsibility, of being aware of those around us, of living in harmony with the human and the more-than-human, of performing rituals and ceremonies.[4]

American Indian works of art are not just of the present but timeless in that artistic creation and consumption, like life itself, is fully dependent on continuing to create a world for past, present, and future ancestors. Herein lies yet another parameter of Native aesthetics: the world is in a state of creation, and each person is part of the continual creation, rather than a historical recounting or reenactment.

Too often, others have determined and provided new meanings for Native American art. For better or for worse, well-meaning European and American patronage has frequently influenced both its content and its form. Today, for example, contemporary Native artists face the dilemma of satisfying the twin demands of tradition and audience; these demands have created multiple codings of their work that must respond to various systems of aesthetics. Similarly, in many representations of bodies of historical Native American art, discussions have been the work of non-Native scholars, who have consistently felt compelled to recontextualize and provide meanings. In much of the discourse about and analysis of Native art generated by non-Indians, little or no attention has been paid to the existence of a Native exegesis, which has been believed to be nonexistent or inaccessible or to have died with Native cultures. Furthermore, many commentators have believed there is some universal aesthetic that could be known and applied to any art; others believed that Native people, diminished and marginalized, had nothing to say about their own art and its production. Nevertheless, Native intellectual precepts today continue to live in Native artists and their work, as well as in historical Indian art. As Ho-Chunk artist and curator Truman Lowe has said: "The visual aspects of these objects are very complete. The connections between the art and Native people are all still there. We are still Indian people. Even if the object is of a historical nature, we as Indian people are the connection." Art is never old, never passé; rather, it is dynamic and continually evolving.

The particular challenge of this exhibition and publication is to return Native American art to its culture of origin and its families, to examine the qualities that are significant in its making, and to lessen the objecthood that has burdened our understandings of Native art. Although some believe that the non-Native world already appreciates and understands Native art, Native people have been largely excluded from the dialogues and debates. Often, for example, Native art has been reinterpreted and sentimentalized to serve as an antidote to European-American society's own longings and ills. As well, Native American art studies has tended to be insular in addressing its own audiences about its own production of scholarship. Native-made art is the original American art, the first American art, which needs to take its place in the contexts of art historical studies rather than continue to be marginalized into studies of the Other or only as a source of influence for or affinity with European-American art.

In this catalogue, aware of the pitfalls, we seek to produce a new approach, one that is respectful of the good scholarship that has preceded us yet that seeks to establish the presence of Native voice—as represented in the concepts of authority, representation, perspective, and visuality. Historically, exhibitions of American Indian art have been framed within cultural contexts and functionality. In view of recent studies of American Indian aesthetic principles and related moral and spiritual values,[5] there is good reason to emphasize the formal aesthetic aspects of objects along with the moral and religious or spiritual ideas they express. Today we can say there are areas of overlap with other philosophical discourses such as those surrounding sovereignty, environmental ethics, and subjectivity. This more inclusionary approach thus seeks to locate the aesthetic principles and ideas the artists themselves adhered to when producing the art.

Our premise for this exhibition and catalogue, then, is to strip away preconceived notions and previous work and return the object—unfettered and unaltered—to the texts of its original making. "Text" in this instance, from the Latin *texere* (to weave), informs our usage, with an emphasis on text as an open and unfinished process. It is only through such a return that we will be able to see the piece as the maker intended it and the suggested cultural meanings. We

have been less concerned about cultural standards and the telling of one tribe's work from the next and more about the larger, compelling issues of analyzing art. We have sought throughout the project, then, to reestablish or uncover existing systems, placing aside other understandings. If we can stand next to the artist and his or her original intent, then our appreciations should grow exponentially. We will then have better and more complete insights into other cultures and their histories, identities, and philosophies. There is much to be cautious about in promulgating this approach, in particular maintaining the individuality of the hundreds of indigenous cultures while searching for some commonalities. As we have suggested, ultimately Native peoples' relation to the land, as well as some shared history, are the most knowable of their bonds to one another. The exhibition and catalogue should, therefore, be understood as part of a conversation with Native art and artists across time and space at the center of which is the issue of indigenous intellectualism about aesthetics.

To reestablish these critical meanings, we invited Native and non-Native artists, curators, and scholars to discuss the possibility of a new paradigm to use in articulating Native art through an understanding of an American Indian aesthetic: Arthur Amiotte (Lakota), Janet Berlo, J. J. Brody, Robert Davidson (Haida), Frank Ettawageshik (Odawa), Harry Fonseca (Maidu), Tom Hill (Seneca), and Peter Macnair; and, from the NMAI's staff, Bruce Bernstein, Emil Her Many Horses (Lakota), Mary Jane Lenz, Truman Lowe (Ho-Chunk), Gerald McMaster (Plains Cree), and Ann McMullen. Fonseca stated the possibilities when he said, "I would like just to put our own things out—not done by others, not interpreted by others—but rather to talk about aesthetics non-verbally, so people can sense [the power and beauty of the objects]." Amiotte suggested that visitors should be given the space in which to see beauty and experience perfection in each piece.

By challenging preexisting notions through their collecting and display of Native art in their New York City home alongside Mark Rothko, Louise Nevelson, Helen Frankenthaler, and other late-twentieth-century American and European artists, Charles and Valerie Diker support the shift of conversations about Native-made art away from the ethnologized discussions of otherness to one that amounts to an almost modernist formalism. The Dikers' setting of disparate artworks together, each on its own terms, shows that they appreciate the objet d'art regardless of who made it. Though their Native art collection is beautiful, we knew that further investigation would uncover what artist and educator Ettawageshik called "the mechanisms of production," in other words, "one which ensures us that we are seeing the pieces in the present and future and that this is not to be a retrospective on Indian art, but rather on how the indigenous has been and will continue to be an essential part of people's lives." To meet in their home, surrounded by their collection, was the surest and quickest method by which to immerse our curatorial group in the Dikers' vision, a place to begin the conversation.

The direction the group came up with was to explicate an existing system or order in which to organize the exhibition and to inform visitors about the culturally based aesthetic systems within the art. Following are seven assumptions or principles that will facilitate a new basis on which to articulate an indigenous aesthetic, one that will give you, the reader, entry into this complex field. These ideas are the outcome of the meeting of the team of artists and scholars, Native and non-Native, in New York City at the Dikers' home in April 2003. The two other essayists who appear in this book—Margaret Dubin and Donald Kuspit—also were present, and they gave their perspectives on the subject of collecting and abstraction, respectively. We have taken

these conversations and honed them according to each of our understandings of Native art—one of us as a practicing Native artist and curator, the other as a non-Native curator. The following principles of an indigenous aesthetic—*idea, emotion, intimacy, movement, integrity, vocabulary,* and *composition*—should be considered a new facet of this exciting field.

IDEA

The most fleeting of the seven principles is *idea*. It is by far the most abstract of them all, yet it encompasses all of them. Truman Lowe says that objects relate to one another not as things but rather as ideas, "[telling the viewer] this is what [the artists] were thinking about; this is what they were experiencing." An idea can be individual or shared, representative of an event or abstract. In some cases, an idea is a recalled image or picture based on an experience. Objects can represent an idea, while at other times they are the idea. Nonetheless, they are signs; thus, objects don't mean, people mean. We need interpretations of what objects mean to particular people at specific moments. One moment they are third-person objects, the next they are first-person subjects. Over time, however, objects' meanings inevitably change; like palimpsests, their meanings are continually erased and reinscribed. Although meanings shift, art is nevertheless symbolic or metaphoric of the ideas that underpin and direct societies. The works in the Diker collection were made by highly skilled artists, but those artists were, of course, influenced by their culture and ideology, which colored how they saw, spoke, danced, sang, heard, and felt the world around them. As Davidson reminded our group, "the beauty of the object is its fullness [i.e., its connections to the culture of its origin]. . . . [Expanding] my understanding of the art form meant asking questions of my elders that went beyond their knowledge"; this suggests that artists internalize the cultural system in which they work. Thus, all the works in the Diker collection can be seen to exist within a larger framework. Each object is part of a larger system of knowledge and philosophy that is continually expanding and contracting, a Native American art that is an explicit cosmology—a completion of the universe and an intimate form of presentation of a cosmic idea that aligns the body and the mind with the universe.

Jump Dance basket, c. 1890, artist unknown, Karuk; conifer root, bear grass, maidenhair fern stems, hazel sticks, feathers, 23 × 55 × 17 cm, DAC 588 (cat. no. 15).

Peter Jones, wearing the bag shown at right; Mississauga Ojibwe, 1845. Photograph by David Octavius Hill and Robert Adamson. Courtesy Scottish National Portrait Gallery, Edinburgh, PGPHA.

Bag, c. 1800, artist unknown, Mississauga Ojibwe; hide, porcupine quills, silk, hair, tinned iron, vegetal cordage, glass beads, 35 × 27 × 4 cm, DAC 586 (cat. no. 14).

Artists portray the world of ideas and belief—ideas that are expressed with reference to the visible and invisible world. Without the other six principles offered here—*emotion, intimacy, movement, integrity, vocabulary,* and *composition*—the abstract process of translating ideas into physical form would be nearly impossible. But that may be what is so significant about Native American art. Idea can be understood as the center or context of the cultural milieu, the values that expand and constrain the artist's world. As artist Fonseca looked at a basket in the collection made by Washoe artist Datsolalee (cat. no. 187), he commented that its beauty is the "humanness and involvement . . . and transformation of the world around her into art." Idea, then, is the basis for Datsolalee's baskets. In that her work is distinctive, it includes her individuality, although she used the same materials and techniques as other Washoe and Paiute weavers. Idea is also the quality of Datsolalee making baskets, just as Washoe weavers have done since eternity. The Washoe rationalist view tells us that baskets were part of the creation; therefore there is no sense of evolution and change, but one of continuous idea.

That art is part of a broader cultural system can be seen in a Jump Dance basket (cat. no. 15) that belongs to an entire and proper Jump Dance ceremonial outfit; in blanket strips (cat. nos. 2, 22), which, attached to buffalo robes and worn across the back, creating decorative elements, orient the wearer and viewer to his or her cosmological position; and in containers for the simple acts of serving or holding food or water that are metaphoric of and therefore become the cosmos (cat. nos. 3–6, 12). The Cheyenne baby moccasins (cat. no. 13) are unusual in that the soles are completely beaded; most moccasins had unbeaded soles of rawhide or moose hide. Hardly intended to be worn regularly, this unusual footwear was lovingly made by someone (mother, grandmother, aunt) for a baby. Animal and bird designs adorn the top side, or vamp, and the same bird form appears underneath. On the vamp the bird is beaded so that it appears to face the wearer. The bird on the underside flies within a dark blue, almost nighttime sky, while the other flies in a white sky. What is the idea within this rather innocent work? There are perhaps many. One is *preciousness.* The artist's idea here might have been to create something for someone she cherished.

The more-than-human is an important idea according to which human beings relate to a world populated by spiritual forces. The Mississauga Ojibwe bag (cat. no. 14; pictured above, worn at left by Peter Jones) has on it three images: Turtle, Thunderbird, and a human.[6] All the forms come together to express an idea. The idea is more than a simple narrative about the power of Thunderbird, the story

Pipe (left, detail), c. 1820, artist
unknown, Eastern or Great Lakes;
pipestone, wood, 4 × 29.5 × 2 cm,
DAC 722 (cat. no. 24). *Pipe* (right,
detail), c. 1820, artist unknown,
Eastern or Great Lakes; pipestone,
wood, 4 × 29 × 2 cm, DAC 721
(cat. no. 23).

of origin in which Turtle is central, or the human being's relationship to the cosmos. The bag must be viewed as a whole, the sum of the various parts. That whole tells the viewer something about the wearer's or holder's own personal and family position toward creation itself. The wavy lines that surround them, even the hair hanging from the bottom, are often associated with spiritual power; here they seem to separate the forms from the human world. The flap's more abstract design completes the composition. The flap begins at the jagged edge immediately above the figures, and each major or minor chevron shape points directly toward or emanates from each figure. The central Thunderbird holds the power position. The other two minor figures, which have tufts of red hair held together by metal cones, are equals on the receiving end of the power that emanates from Thunderbird toward them. Across the top a band of colors—red and white—forms white circles. Two circles, possibly the sun and moon, straddle Thunderbird. In fact, all the circles are potentially celestial in this bag, which is so full of power that it begins to form a spiritual universe. The artist laid down the brightly colored quill and beadwork images on a black hide background, which adds further drama. The power, or wavy, lines running across the side and along the bottom are a sign of the water Ojibwe life centers on. These wavy lines may point to the underwater serpent Mishapishoo, Thunderbird's great opposing force; together they are always in struggle with each other. Thus the bag gives us a picture of the kinds of more-than-human relations many Native cultures have had and continue to have with the spiritual forces around us.

The Ako (Acoma) olla, or water jar (cat. no. 5), was created to carry water from the community cistern to a family's home. The olla was made and used at a time when people entered and exited their homes through the roof; a woman probably carried it on her head while climbing up and down ladders. The vessel was intended to be seen in motion, being carried and in use in the village, as well as in the ever changing and shifting landscape that embraces the Acoma world. Without a doubt, then, it is also imbued with Puebloan cosmology. The olla itself is made of earth—the mud of the very substance and creation of the First People. Mud is used to plaster homes; it is also used to decorate dancers on ceremonial days. If and when an olla breaks, the shards are often returned to the earth; some celebrate that the clay is once again free. Other shards are ground into temper to be incorporated into new pots. Understood in this way, while we might suggest that the pot is a clay or ceramic vessel, it is really made of the fertile substance from which life itself is created. Procreation is part of the larger consciousness of Pueblo people and their persistence in and insistence on living in the dry high desert climate of the American Southwest. The iconography on pottery is also about procreation—the plants and birds on this pot invoke the results of rain. The clouds and moisture symbols bring rain and are the result of rain, and, on this pottery jar, they are rain. Birds fly in the clouds from which rain comes, carrying prayers for rain skyward. The appearance of green plants in New Mexico's high desert environment is a direct result of rain; the appearance of these plants on this pottery jar is an invocation for rain and the green plants that result.

The Chumash coin bowl (cat. no. 8), originally made for presentation by the Spanish to other non-indigenous visitors to Upper California in the second decade of the nineteenth century, is decorated with a Spanish double real coin motif. The basket is the work of a Chumash weaver, Lapulimeu, whose individual hand prepared the materials and plied her technique. Certainly, this bowl makes a strong case that the core idea of Chumash baskets remained unchanged despite the incorporation of new designs and uses.

As Ettawageshik reminded our curatorial group, Indian art is a dynamic force, something that allows people to survive and thrive, not an art that is timeless, romantic, and of the past. Idea prevails above all else in indigenous art: it overcomes the cultural change and integration, it overcomes the physical and psychological separation from homelands and kin, and, ultimately, it soars above the ages, providing a clear and articulate means of continuance. Ultimately, idea relates to the appreciation of the specific circumstances of Native art, whose character and spirit was formed by a tenure of millennia in the landscape of North America.

EMOTION

An expression or exclamation of pleasure, a strong feeling toward something, is an aspect of the aesthetic in which the viewer has some form of emotional response, an expression of sensual cognition, feeling, or sensation. Objects will be beautiful where materials and ideas combine to produce an object that speaks to the viewer on the level of *emotion*. In this case, the immediacy of expression evokes a response that can be called the "gasp factor." As scholar Janet Berlo suggested, "How do we get beyond identity politics and have an unbiased appreciation of these art works? [In other words,] it's okay for everyone to be enthralled [by] an object. . . ." The extraordinary beauty of good art elicits an emotional response, an exclamation of the beauty, or perhaps the artist has captured a moment in time, a piece of light, or an event exactly as you, the observer and appreciator, also remember. Ettawageshik explained this as "cross-cultural" and "timeless," meaning the "continuity of human experience . . . it speaks of the future, it speaks of the present, and it speaks of the past." We all agreed that we often have a "gasp" reaction to beholding an object and its magnificence. Only later will we want to know more about it, to assimilate its contents; but this is intellectual and more about ratiocination. As Fonseca opined, "The gasp is good enough; we don't need to explain it further."

Images provide sometimes joy, sometimes the collective investment of understanding one's own position in the cosmos in relation to the animal beings represented in these objects. It is these associations that make us as viewers want to dance around an object, to celebrate its existence. The immediacy of the imagery creates this emotion, as can the realization that a family member made the basket. Artist Amiotte, for example, shared his high emotions when he spotted a muslin painting (cat. no. 84) by his grandfather,

Standing Bear (Lakota), South Dakota, c. 1919. Photograph by Louis R. Bostwick, Omaha, Nebraska, file 67. Courtesy Arthur Amiotte.

Battle of the Little Bighorn (detail), c. 1920, Standing Bear, Lakota; cotton, ink, pencil, watercolor, 96 × 265 cm, DAC 652 (cat. no. 84).

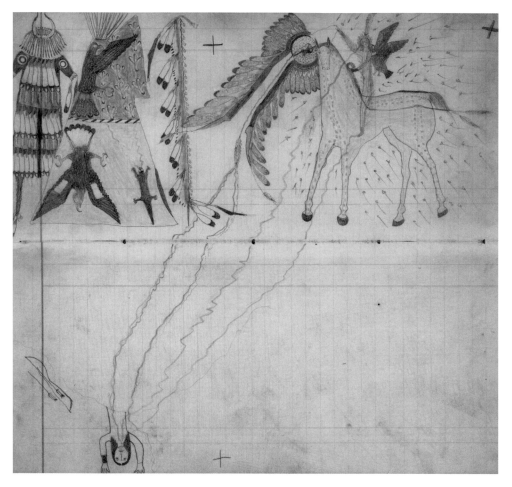

Medicine Vision (detail), c. 1882, Henderson Ledger Artist A, Arapaho; pencil, colored pencil, ink, 27 × 30 cm, DAC 024LD (cat. no. 27).

Standing Bear (pictured on p. 43), in the Dikers' apartment. The honor songs Joseph No Two Horns sang to his shield (cat. no. 55) may be long silent, but the pride and singularity he enjoyed is evident in it. When seen within the context of the shield's making, our emotional response, best expressed as appreciation, is heightened. Ceremonies, especially public presentations, can stimulate any number of emotions, such as excitement, fear, joy, and rage. In contemporary times, for example, the powwow brings out emotional highs in both dancers and spectators, especially during competition. Some Northwest Coast presentations may instill theatrical fear, not to intimidate the audience, but rather to engage them. When objects are involved in ceremonies, they can add to the emotional impact. The annual ceremonial appearance of a Raven rattle is always bound to cause some excitement, giving a sense of theatricality to express the emotional moment. The person holding the rattle holds it with Raven beneath, in other words, upside down; it is said that this prevents Raven from flying out of one's hand. Since Raven is in most if not all Northwest Coast cultures a cultural hero, the one who was there at the beginning of time and the one who brought them their traditions, representations are particularly sensitive to the many conditions Raven expresses.

At the time this simple but elegant upper Missouri or Northern Plains blanket strip (cat. no. 56) was made, beads were an exotic and exciting new medium. Curator and artist Emil Her Many Horses marveled at "the vision that she [the artist] had . . . [in that] she got [the] beauty of two colors and reflected light." Her Many Horses mused, "How do you work with just two colors? It is very difficult today when we are so familiar with beads; but how did she do [it] when beads were new and unknown? The strip is also contemporary, but can you imagine how new it must have been in 1830 when it was originally made?"

The drawing *Medicine Vision*, by Henderson Ledger Artist A (cat. no. 27), emotes a particular state of consciousness. The only human being in the image appears in an upside-down position in the lower panel; this position often signifies death, but, in this case, it indicates the man's altered state of consciousness—that is, his position between this world and the next. The lines signify that he is drawing energy from his vision of the shield and the figure on horseback. When the image is viewed upside down, the man appears to be standing on a hill, arms raised, with his bow and arrows alongside him. We may be able to surmise that if the warrior makes a new shield in the manner received in the vision and paints his horse with similar designs, both will be spiritually protected from bullets and other deadly projectiles.

INTIMACY

The idea of *intimacy* is multiple. Generally it is about close relations between people who know each other very well—a loved one, a close relative, a lover—where certain formalities can be dispensed with, since there is some understanding of why such a relation exists. As a value often overlooked in Native American art, it has enormous potential as an aid to understanding many works. Intimacy is suggested in the use of objects; a flute, for example, played for a lover carries many long-lasting thoughts between them. The giving of gifts can hold many unspoken thoughts carried by the heart. Intimacy is also about the relationship of the maker to the art and of the user to the art. The decoration on the surface might be covered during use or so small or intricate that no one other than those using or holding the piece can view it adequately (see, for example, cat. nos. 64, 77, 79).

Crooked knife (detail), c. 1840, artist unknown, Algonquin Mocotaugan(?), possibly Delaware; wood, steel, shellac, 33 × 4 × 2 cm, DAC 725 (cat. no. 86).

Indigenous art often depends on decorated surfaces that change through being carried or used. Amanda Wilson's acorn sifting tray (cat. no. 78) is decorated with quail plumes that are covered up when the basket is in use. The woman sees the design as she covers it with the meal to be sifted and sees it again as it is revealed as she sifts the meal from the tray. Each partial uncovering reveals the quail underneath, which from differing angles appear to be running or flying, individually, in pairs, or in groups. Indigenous art is both individual and privileged. In museums we place an object such as a rattle in close proximity to the visitor in order to provide him or her with an intimate viewing experience,

whereas in its original context, it was taken out and used only one time per year, when it was seen by the audience from ten or more feet away. Macnair suggests that the rattle is in that original context a "cloistered piece, intimate to the performer and just a few others." Intimacy relates not only to limited access to the piece but also to what it means. The Ute baby carrier (cat. no. 75) holds countless moments of our mothers. In this work, the mother's love is resplendently displayed, from the magnificent and expressive beadwork to the care with which the baby is enveloped by the pouch; only the child's head appears, and the baby's arms are tucked tightly against his or her sides. The tightly held cover made of twigs bends over the top to shield the head. The designs dance around the head on a golden ground, only to be held back by the surrounding and much more severe design that runs all the way around, as if to provide protection, both spiritual and emotional. The baby is covered by art and embraced with love. The cradle is constructed to surround the baby with beauty. It can also contain private, intimate moments between a mother and child.

The ledger drawings done by nineteenth-century warrior-artists on the Plains are among the most original expressions that continue to be copied by a new generation of contemporary artists. The older works address issues of intimacy, whereas today's are marketed more to the public. In the past warrior-artists expressed the private and personal through what they drew, filling ledger books with images that are highly personal and touching in their intimacy, such as *Wives Honoring Husbands* (cat. no. 87) by a Kiowa artist, which represents a public ceremony that expresses intimacy between loved ones. The ceremony belongs both to the Kiowa and to the individuals involved. In a culture in which privacy was almost a non-existent concept because everyone lived so close to one another—in which everything was shared, honored, and celebrated—intimacy was expressed in many ways that contradict privacy.

Most of us are outsiders to indigenous art—whether because we are non-Indian or from another tribe. Privilege comes with intimacy if the maker is a relative or from the cultural circumstances that continue to bind Native communities together, such as when the Amanda Wilson tray is made by Fonseca's great-aunt, or Amiotte finds in the Diker collection a painted muslin made by his grandfather.

Dogfish frontlet, c. 1860, artist unknown, Haida; wood, paint, abalone, 20 × 16 × 5 cm, DAC 540 (cat. no. 136).

Intimacy is also an element of Davidson's relationship to the Haida frontlet (cat. no. 136)—a lifetime of experience of making, wearing, and seeing them in use for which there is no substitute. His intimate relation with Haida art provides what he terms an "artistic freedom—because the intimate meanings of art are known and used." Intimacy is vital to the appreciation of indigenous art on its own terms, rather than through systems imposed by those who might know little of its origins. That intimacy can come from being related to an artist or from sharing the same culture. Consciousness of the intimate relationship of the maker to her or his culture is also important to an understanding of indigenous art; through it, we can gain an understanding of the factors of technique, materials, and artistic impulse and, further,

recognize that old and new sources are continually adjusted, incorporated, and discarded.

MOVEMENT

All works have some capacity for *movement:* to move, to be moved, or to be seen as moving. Much of Native art has to be seen in motion in order to understand and appreciate its kinetic qualities, for example, in its use in the dance. Art is an integral element of many functional objects, whose patterns shift and collide when they are shaken and moved (for example, cat. no. 94). Rock art is created on rock canvases that appear to vault into the sky or are placed against a background of changing patterns of sunlight and seasons, affecting our appreciation and understanding. Pomo and Maidu basket designs (see cat. nos. 100, 107) are meant to continue to rise above the rim of the finished basket—moving outward indefinitely—and Western Apache and Karuk baskets (cat. nos. 99, 108) are created to be demonstratively mobile as well as to hold in focus a bit of the cosmos's constant motion.

Like all baby carriers, the Kiowa baby carrier (cat. no. 102), whose cradleboard moves and colors sway, was, when not stationary, carried on a mother's back. From the carrier, the child saw the world move by from the same height as an adult, and when he or she was set down, it was usually in an upright position, often in a high place such as a tree; the world was seen from a lower perspective only after a child began to walk. The Crow boy's shirt (cat. no. 101) exemplifies the idea of movement in the lives of Plains people. Fringes hang from the beadwork sewn along the soft deerskin arms, shoulders, and chest. Softly falling to the ground like the distant rain or hail on the prairies, the fringes seem innocent. An extension of the body, the fringe, like hair, can represent some form of precipitation, an element that relates sky to earth in an act of procreation. The leftover skin not used in the sewing together of sections of the garment is used to make the irregular fringes. It is cut very, very thinly, which allows weight to be evenly distributed; the longer it is, the further the swing or pendulum movement. Contemporary female dancers take great pride in using an economy of movement, which allows fringes to swing effortlessly back and forth, in complete rhythm with body movement and drum beat.

Fringe was hung from both men's and women's clothing, sometimes in a show of honor, or in a show of pride in war, or to make small sounds, or to suggest spirituality. The four winds were a constant on the flat plains and prairies, and works with kinetic qualities were created in response to the winds' power; various forms express this important and powerful relation, whether it is fringe, feathers, the aerodynamically shaped tipi, the warrior on horseback, or the simple style of living that disallowed accumulation, making it easier to be on the move. Lightness and movement exemplified the lifestyle of the Plains people.

The Lakota Grass Dance whistle (cat. no. 76) in the form of a bird's head says it all. Its open beak announces its tune, its voice, and its identity. A bit of fur separates its head from the whistle's stem; both are colored separately.

Sally bag, c. 1900, artist unknown, Wasco; native hemp, corn husks, 30 × 17.5 cm, DAC 719 (cat. no. 119).

A simple placement of a white bead stands for the eye. Its simplicity echoes so much the Plains lifestyle and its cultures. It is not a whistle that delivers any melodic tune; rather it is more sonorous, a single birdlike sound that is to draw attention to its blower. At today's powwows, for example, dancers will carry whistles, usually eagle bone, and on occasions when a song is particularly good and the entire arena of dancers feel inspired, a male dancer will approach the drum and blow his whistle, usually four times, signaling the drumming and singing to continue. If no one blows again to keep the music going, the singing stops and the blower will approach the drum group and reward them with a small gift, usually cash.

INTEGRITY

Integrity is the character of individuals as artists and their relation to cultural heritage over time and to the world around them, both human and more-than-human, and the relation among them, their traditional media, and the level of mastery they must reach in order to articulate both idea and form (*vocabulary*). Integrity helps us realize why we have indigenous art in spite of the cultural change and colonization that Native peoples have experienced and how Native people have survived and persisted in the face of genocidal policies. While suffering from the ignorance of prejudice and governmental policies designed to undermine their cultures, Native peoples created great art, as is evidenced in this exhibition and catalogue. These artists fit

their work into ancient traditions, though all around them their worlds were changing.

Maria and Julian Martinez of San Ildefonso Pueblo, New Mexico, are two such seminal artists. This husband-and-wife team, through the development and refinement of modern Pueblo art pottery styles, established a niche in broader society through work that secured their own cultural traditions and practices. An olla made by them in the winter of 1919–20 (cat. no. 123) marks the closing of almost a decade of experimentation and visionary ceramic work. Their collaborative work transformed a hard-use and high-fired common ware used by Pueblo people to a deep, lustrous black, polished form worthy of display in anyone's home or a museum.

The water serpent, or Avanyu, that encircles the pot is part of the Pueblos' oral tradition. Although the artists fully relied upon existing technologies, materials, and designs, in order to create a future for their destitute village, they combined them in new and profound ways, creating new understandings and potentials for Pueblo art and culture. It was the integrity of their culture that made possible the fusion of the ancient art of pottery making with the making of a wholly new style of art pottery for the non-Pueblo world. This couple used art to bring recognition, pride, and a much-needed cash economy to a village losing land and all of its water rights. Both of them had been raised in an environment where they were either directly or indirectly told that being an Indian was not good. Today's

Grass Dance whistle, c. 1870, artist unknown, Lakota; wood, fur, pigment, beads, cotton thread, 76 × 4 × 4 cm, DAC 462 (cat. no. 76).

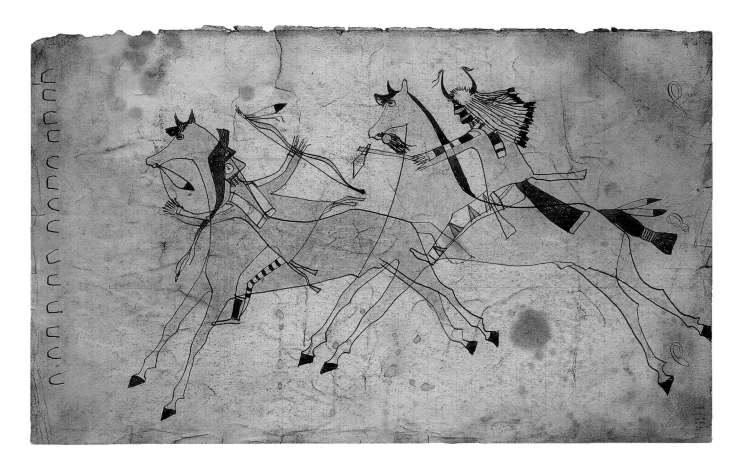

admiration and appreciation for Native cultures is in no small way a result of the integrity of the pottery they created. In *Swift Dog in Pursuit of a Mounted Crow Warrior* (cat. no. 121), a ledger drawing—so-called because artists from the Plains often used odd media on which to create drawings—you will see lines running vertically and the number "169" on the lower right, two signs that betray its origin in a discarded accountant's book. This medium, like so many materials that originated from European sources, was promptly engaged into the warrior cultures because it afforded various warrior-artists an opportunity to illuminate their personal narratives. So while on one hand, the idea of *integrity* was in the materials used, on the other it was in the truthfulness of the storyteller.

Another idea of integrity would be how the warrior-artist tells his story. It is one thing to tell a story about something that involved no witnesses—such as fictional situations, jokes, and tall tales; it is quite another to tell a story about an event in which people were witness to the actions of the teller, who often gains honors through his credibility. In this drawing, Swift Dog, the protagonist and artist, is closing in on his target and thrusting his hatchet toward him, either killing or embarrassing his opponent by merely touching him, an act called *coup*. The warrior-artist must have his story corroborated by his fellow warriors over campfires; afterward, he can depict his actions in drawings or paintings.

The Plains Miwok of Central California suffered almost total annihilation through warfare, disease, and missionization in Spanish California. Nonetheless, a few pieces of their basketry have survived (see cat. no. 138), testament to the integrity of the cultural systems they developed and the sustainability of those systems in scarce singular pieces of art. Other pieces in this section also illustrate the integrity of art in the face of tremendous change.

Artists such as Lucy Telles (see cat. no. 127) and Nampeyo (see cat. no. 124) are increasingly appreciated as visionary for their fine artistry, but their technique and materials also have the integrity of being part of a long continuous tradition. It is their evolving practice of these artistic traditions that exemplifies integrity. Telles, who lived the greater portion of her life in Yosemite National Park, integrated two styles of baskets—both of which were of her heritage—to create new baskets to be collected by non-Indians. She, like Nampeyo from the village of Polacca on First Mesa at Hopi, was the subject of tourism and of the accompanying sentimentality and admiration that visitors heaped upon them. Nonetheless, in an era when people generally did not differentiate between one artist and the next, Telles and Nampeyo became known artists. Both were able to do this because their work is so demonstratively connected to their own tradition as well as being modern and innovative; these qualities point to integrity.

Swift Dog in Pursuit of a Mounted Crow Warrior, c. 1870, Swift Dog, Hunkpapa Lakota; paper, ink, watercolor, 21 × 34 cm, DAC 169LD (cat. no. 121).

VOCABULARY

Tribal *vocabulary* can be seen as a set of expressive forms used in an art. For each tribe there exist such vocabularies, each understood and articulated by artists. Sometimes they belong to a discourse that outsiders must learn before they can become initiated. To understand such a vocabulary is to apprehend experiences or to express ideas or feelings. Artists have to assimilate and understand before they have complete facility to be creative, not necessarily "breaking the rules," but rather introducing a new way of looking. Native people were open to the reception of new ideas and materials, yet they were always assimilating these to their purposes, based on their local vocabulary. The Diker collection is rife with examples that maintain vocabulary yet easily absorb others.

Vocabulary is a culture's way of understanding and giving meaning to the environment; it is a sum total of its history, predictable or unpredictable, strange or well known. Yet it is often incomprehensible to outsiders because language and vocabulary are generally understandable only to those within a culture. The potential still exists for us to understand how the Haida horn spoon (cat. no. 162) relates to the culture from which it originates, because the Haida continue to live on the same islands and still have their aboriginal language, their clan system of relationships, their customs and traditions of potlatch, and artists who produce great works of art such as this. Although Haida history over the last centuries has been difficult, their cultural recovery has been remarkable. Artists have trained themselves well to understand Haida artistic vocabulary, which enables them to recognize what an object such as this means to their culture.

Just as the prospective artist must know the formal principles of art—form, line, texture, and so on—before he or she can manipulate or control the medium, that artist must learn a cultural vocabulary before proceeding to the making of an object. Certainly it is possible to make baskets without knowing this vocabulary, but their meaning will not then be understood. One aspect of tribal visual vocabulary is the idea that a basket is "a song made visible."[7] Like baskets, songs tell stories: they give meaning to the surrounding world and tell of the many relations between plant, animal, and human beings and the cosmos, past and present. Both help people remember; both represent ideas. Objects such as the lidded jar (cat. no. 158) by Elizabeth Hickox (pictured at far right) bind these worlds of meanings together, both as discrete objects and in their ceremonial use. In cases such as these, ideas are more important than the materiality, since objects can be remade over and over again, by many artists, generation after generation. What is powerful is the idea. Unfortunately, when songs die and are forgotten, so do their meanings, and all that is left is the object, without life. The songs give it life, putting it into motion. When meanings are lost, then baskets become objects. To believers, however, they are more than objects. They are subjects; in other words, they carry meaning and are usually referenced in the first person when used in ceremony, although many objects are used for non-ceremonial, quotidian purposes.

Horn spoon (detail), c. 1850, artist unknown, Haida; horn, shell, copper, 28 × 8 × 26 cm, DAC 506 (cat. no. 162).

In many Native American cultures, materials have qualities to which cultures attach particular kinds of meanings. Whether it is sweet grass, cedar, wood, clay, or pipestone, certain media have religious or spiritual as well as secular purposes and meanings. Animals in particular have specific meanings attached to them, both in the qualities of their being and in their tactility or organicity. Thus the medium is often an essential part of Native representational vocabulary.

The Innu man's summer coat (cat. no. 160) is an example of how vocabularies can come into contact with one another and be incorporated into the local artistic dialect without destroying its essential foundations. Although the materials—skin and paint—are entirely Innu, the tailoring is very European. The abstract designs are consistently local, as were the painting tools used to create the designs, and the tanned hide is consistent with local techniques, yet the infusion of new ideas, such as European tailoring, has strengthened the vocabulary.

The Lakota(?) baby moccasins (cat. no. 167), unlike the Cheyenne beaded-soled moccasins (cat. no. 13), are made of quilled hide. An abstract symmetrical pattern covers them in what may be a star design. But today it is difficult to understand how they represent a particular vocabulary. As a sign, they are only partial; most older objects are today incomplete signs, the complete signs having existed somewhere in the past, in the original cultural context of its user or wearer. Today the moccasins function as artifact, a representation of their past or of the wearer's culture, and

our understanding of their vocabulary can only be partial at best.

The moccasin is the perfect footwear for walking on the earth, for not only does it conform perfectly to one's foot, it is also in perfect alignment with the natural elements. Unlike hard-soled shoes, the moccasin would wear out very quickly on the hard surfaces found on modern streets and in buildings. In virtually every collection, large or small, there is bound to be a pair of moccasins; their ubiquity is mind-boggling. Every imaginable type, size, shape, color, and design seem to exist, and it would be truly remarkable to see them all together. Men, women, and children wore them; many were not worn by Native people but were made for non-Indian buyers who also wore them or put them on display as souvenirs or curios. In the National Museum of the American Indian alone, there are well over two thousand pairs, from the Arctic to the desert. Perhaps because they wore out quickly, one might wear several pairs each year; nevertheless each pair was always lovingly decorated and matched to the identity of its wearer.

With so many extant examples in collections worldwide, the language of the shoe would seem to be a common dialect. It is possible that such a dialect exists, but only in museological or scholarly terms. Though Native peoples continue to make various types of footwear, the very best articulations have been so far removed from practice since the late nineteenth century that today the language of moccasins is strangely anachronistic. Yet their resonance filters into our consciousness in strange and unpredictable ways.

Lidded jar, c. 1910, Elizabeth Conrad Hickox, Karuk; hazel shoots, conifer root, maidenhair fern stem, bear grass, 19 × 23 cm, DAC 445 (cat. no. 158).

Elizabeth Conrad Hickox (1875–1947, Karuk; at left) and her daughters, Klamath River, California, c. 1905. Photograph by Grace Nicholson. National Museum of the American Indian, Smithsonian Institution, P28169.

Elizabeth Hickox's family helped her prepare her basketry materials.

Parfleches, c. 1890, artist unknown, Lakota; rawhide, glass beads, pigment, 68 × 33.7 × 8 cm each, DAC 716 (cat. no. 207).

This pair, for example, beautifully quilled, has lost a bit of its original bright colors, yet we can almost sense they were worn not long ago; as with so many other pairs, a trace of its wearer has been left behind.

COMPOSITION

In Native American art, the principle of *composition,* that of putting together elements into a unified whole, is different from the principle of the same name in Western art as there is no coherent written or spoken discourse on it as a whole—only specific cultural discourses. A work of art is like a language, with its own compositional elements that are contained within cultural frameworks—language, environment, religion, cosmology, philosophy, and so on. Anthropology, a discipline that looks beneath surfaces, particularly formalistic surfaces, can help us understand that language, in that it articulates these compositional elements in ways that fall outside conventional aesthetic discourse. In a mate-

rialist sense, good composition is the flawless combination of materials and techniques. This beauty is created through a balance that is seen and experienced in the finished piece of art. But composition reaches beyond the material form to a higher consciousness, where the art is firmly lodged within the context of its creation and intention.

In the 1960s, various discourses emerged that argued that one could describe any work of art based on formal properties—form, line, texture, color, and so on. Bill Holm, for example, in *Northwest Coast Indian Art: An Analysis of Form,* developed his argument around formalism, not around discursively developed frameworks. Although compositional elements—form, line, color—clearly exist in every work of art, we must go beyond this position to get at the ideas the work represents. The Métis shot pouch (cat. no. 198) is made primarily of native materials—animal hide and porcupine quills—although the dye is of uncertain origin. The blackened hide, fairly common in the Woodlands, provides a wonderful base for the brightly colored quills. The artist took a fairly standard approach of creating symmetry to the left and right, top and bottom. The artist twisted quills around a leather fringe, following an even pattern across, and then at the bottom came back around. The quilled design features the signs of the four directions repeated four times. The abstract designs do not overwhelm the overall composition. In fact, the bag remains restful, with the visual action being carried by the fringed loops. Their crowding makes the bag dance, like many tiny shuffling feet being carried along the simple visual load above them; this contrast is similarly indicated by the darkened background and lighter-colored quillwork.

The Creek bandolier bag (cat. no. 200) is, first of all, an example of an art form that has a wide reach among cultures from Florida through the northeastern United States, most of Canada, and into Alaska. Though each culture has taken the basic pattern, that of a shoulder bag, and adapted it to local use and visuality, the materials are all imported from European sources that were picked up and retranslated by local artists. This bag works off its symmetry: the shoulder strap splays down and out, whereas the bag's flaps reverse that movement; between the two opposing shapes a diamond is created. Again the typical dark background serves as a wonderful ground upon which the brightly colored beads and cloth are overlaid. The abstract designs remain non-representational and still, compositionally, the bag holds up, for the designs dazzle the eye. The orange-tipped ends finish off the visually heavy shoulder strap in a brilliant way.

The seven working principles—*idea*, *emotion*, *intimacy*, *movement*, *integrity*, *vocabulary*, and *composition*—have guided us in looking at Native American art in a new and different way. It is one that centers on particular aesthetic qualities that remain objectively present in all the works in the Diker collection as well as on ideas discursively developed within various Native cultures that influence the creation of beautiful works of art. We hope that future students and scholars will find these principles helpful, particularly as they relate to indigenous philosophies, our understanding of the indigenous experience, and the moral and religious ideas they express.

Notes

1. Quoted in Ruth Phillips, "Art History and the Native-Made Object: New Discourses, Old Differences?" in W. Jackson Rushing III, ed., *Native American Art in the Twentieth Century* (New York: Routledge, 1999), 108.

2. Tom Hill spoke these words at the opening day of our two-day seminar, April 7, 2003.

3. See the introduction to this volume for a fuller explication of this concept.

4. James (Sákéj) Youngblood Henderson, a Chickasaw legal scholar, speaks in "Ayukpachi: Empowering Aboriginal Thought" of an "interactive harmony" that orders the Native universe: "Our elders say that if we are to live in harmony we must accept the beauty and limits of our ecology. We must accept our relationship with the surrounding life forces and ourselves as we are. We must honour diversity as the basic right through respectful behaviours. We must be good and kind to all diversity in the circle of life. We must learn to believe and trust the other life forces, to believe in a life force greater than ourselves that gives everything strength to exist, and to endure through many changes." See Marie Battiste, ed., *Reclaiming Indigenous Voice and Vision* (Vancouver: University of British Columbia Press, 2000), 268–69.

5. See, for example, Janet Catherine Berlo, *Plains Indian Drawings, 1865–1935: Pages from a Visual History* (New York: Harry N. Abrams, 1996); Janet Catherine Berlo and Ruth B. Phillips, *Native North American Art* (Oxford and New York: Oxford University Press, 1998); Steven C. Brown, *Native Visions: Evolution in Northwest Coast Art from the Eighteenth through the Twentieth Century* (Seattle: Seattle Art Museum in association with University of Washington Press, 1998); Steven Leuthold, *Indigenous Aesthetics: Native Art, Media, and Identity* (Austin: University of Texas Press, 1998); Ruth B. Phillips, *Patterns of Power: The Jasper Grant Collection and Great Lakes Indian Art of the Early Nineteenth Century* (Kleinburg, Ont.: McMichael Canadian Art Collection, 1984); and Edwin L. Wade, ed., *The Arts of the North American Indian: Native Traditions in Evolution* (New York: Hudson Hills Press, 1986).

6. "In these pouches were carried charms relating to hunting, as well as pipes and tobacco, for both charms and tobacco smoke played a role in the cultivation of a beneficial relationship with the spirits of the wild animals. While occupied with such ritual preparations for the hunt, the owner placed the pouch in front of him like an icon." In Gilbert T. Vincent, Sherry Brydon, and Ralph T. Coe, eds., *Art of the North American Indians: The Thaw Collection* (Seattle: University of Washington Press, 2000), 64.

7. See Tom Hill and Richard W. Hill, Sr., eds., *Creation's Journey: Native American Identity and Belief* (Washington, D.C.: Smithsonian National Museum of the American Indian and Smithsonian Institution Press, 1994), 155.

Catalogue

THE CHARLES AND VALERIE DIKER COLLECTION
OF AMERICAN INDIAN ART

Idea

IDEA TELLS US THAT A CULTURAL SYSTEM OF BELIEFS EXISTS through which artists perceive and interpret the world. It is a deeply rooted intellectualism that continually uses established knowledge—using it as it has always existed as well as reshaping and reformulating it—and that incorporates new ideas and materials.

Objects can represent ideas, and at times they are the idea. Each object is part of a larger system of knowledge and philosophy that is continually expanding and contracting. Each piece is a completion of the universe and an intimate presentation of a cosmic idea that aligns the body and the mind with the universe.

Idea can be understood as the context of the cultural milieu, the values that expand and constrain the artist's world. Above all else, idea is the humanness of the artist and his or her work.

Captions by Arthur Amiotte (AA), Kathleen Ash-Milby (KAM), Janet Berlo (JB), Bruce Bernstein (BB), J.J. Brody (JJB), Robert Davidson (RD), Harry Fonseca (HF), Tom Hill (TH), Peter Macnair (PM), Gerald McMaster (GM), and Ann McMullen (AM).

Dimensions are expressed as height × width × depth or, for circular objects, as height × diameter.

Opposite: ***Olla,*** c. 1770, artist unknown, Ako (Acoma); clay, slip, 28 × 31 cm, DAC 310 (cat. no. 5). ***Bag,*** c. 1800, artist unknown, Mississauga Ojibwe; hide, porcupine quills, silk, hair, tinned iron, vegetal cordage, glass beads, 35 × 27 × 4 cm, DAC 586 (cat. no. 14). ***Baby moccasins,*** c. 1830, artist unknown, Cheyenne; hide, glass beads, sinew, pigment, 7 × 6 × 13 cm each, DAC 573 (cat. no. 13). ***Blanket strip,*** c. 1865, artist unknown, Nez Perce(?); hide, glass beads, porcupine quill, copper alloy bells, wool, sinew, 15 × 160 × 3 cm, DAC 690 (cat. no. 22). This page, background: ***Coin bowl,*** c. 1820, Lapulimeu, Chumash; dyed and undyed juncus stems, 18 × 47 cm, DAC 522 (cat. no. 8).

Cat. no. 1

MOCCASINS, c. 1890

Artist unknown, Otoe
Hide, vegetal-tanned hide, glass beads, cotton thread
9 × 9 × 26 cm each
DAC 111

The style of beadwork on these moccasins, called "spot stitch,"
allows an artist the freedom to create semi-abstract and stylized
forms. This new style, which was introduced to the Prairies from
Great Lakes tribes, is characterized by free-flowing designs with
white outlines. This work represents a miniature cosmos of birds
and stars arranged in perfect symmetry. As is often the case with
moccasins, this pair's design would have faced its wearer. —GM

Cat. no. 2

BLANKET STRIP, c. 1875

Artist unknown, Crow
Hide, glass beads, sinew, cotton thread
150 × 19 × 2 cm
DAC 164

Cat. no. 3
SEED JAR, c. 1905

Nampeyo, Hopi
Clay
9 × 22 cm
DAC 240

Cat. no. 4
OLLA, c. 1900

Artist unknown, Acoma
Clay, slip
32 × 32 cm
DAC 306

Cat. no. 5
OLLA, c. 1770
Artist unknown, Ako (Acoma)
Clay, slip
28 × 31 cm
DAC 310

In the Native domestic setting this pot was created for, it would have been seen either being carried atop a person's head or sitting on the floor of a room. The artist was conscious of this and made it to be seen from those two positions. — JJB

Cat. no. 6

TRAY, c. 1880

Artist unknown, Yurok
Conifer root, maidenhair fern
stems, hazel sticks
15 × 59 cm
DAC 424A

Cat. no. 7

SADDLEBAG, c. 1880

Artist unknown, Teton Lakota
Hide, glass beads, tinned iron,
horsehair, sinew
35 × 49 × 17 cm
DAC 435

Cat. no. 8

COIN BOWL, c. 1820

Lapulimeu, Chumash
Dyed and undyed juncus stems
18 × 47 cm
DAC 522

Lapulimeu's grounding in her own culture and its aesthetic
principles is apparent in her skillful adaptation of a Spanish
coin design into Chumash weaving traditions. The presence
of new elements in a culturally specific form is one of the
wonderful aspects of this piece. — BB

Cat. no. 9

DANCE MASK, c. 1905

Artist unknown, Yup'ik
Wood, paint, feathers, vegetal fiber,
sinew, ferrous nails
100 × 67 × 23 cm
DAC 527

Cat. no. 10

ROBE, c. 1875

Artist unknown, Arapaho
Hide, pigment
136 × 165 cm
DAC 530

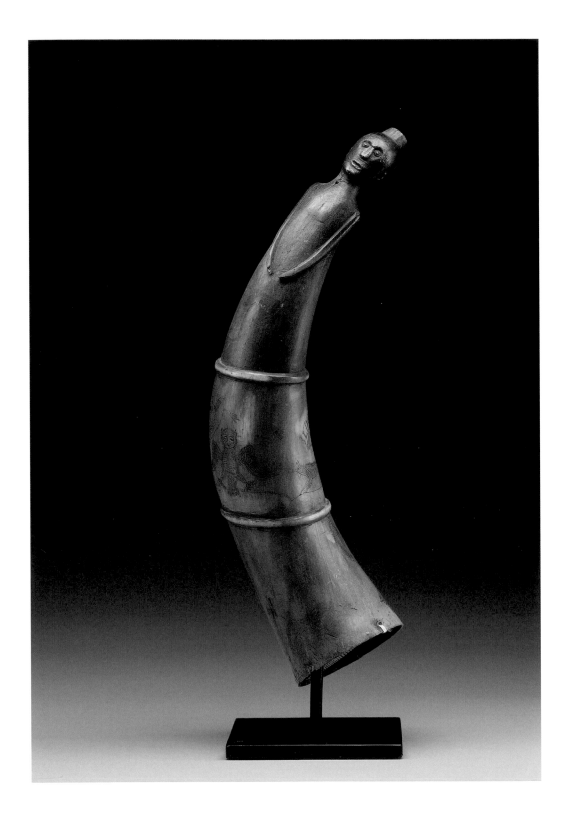

Cat. no. 12

BOWL, c. 1840

Artist unknown, Wishram or Wasco
Wood, pigment(?), nails
17 × 25 cm
DAC 569

Cat. no. 13
BABY MOCCASINS, c. 1830
Artist unknown, Cheyenne
Hide, glass beads, sinew, pigment
7 × 6 × 13 cm each
DAC 573

Beaded-soled moccasins often express dedication to their wearers, be they child or adult. This special feature is understood by others to express a close and loving relationship. The rather unpretentious design expresses a world unknown to the child even while it provides him or her with a special status within the community. —GM

Cat. no. 14

BAG, c. 1800

Artist unknown, Mississauga Ojibwe
Hide, porcupine quills, silk, hair, tinned
iron, vegetal cordage, glass beads
35 × 27 × 4 cm
DAC 586

Even today, more than 150 years after its
creation, the reds and blacks in this bag's
quillwork glow, jumping off the black
background, which was darkened with
black walnut. — KAM

Cat. no. 15

JUMP DANCE BASKET,
c. 1890

Artist unknown, Karuk
Conifer root, bear grass,
maidenhair fern stems,
hazel sticks, feathers
23 × 55 × 17 cm
DAC 588

Cat. no. 16
SHAMAN FIGURE, c. 1870
Artist unknown, Tlingit
Iron, hair, cordage, hide, wool
31 × 7 × 5.5 cm
DAC 614

Cat. no. 17
RATTLE, c. 1880
Artist unknown, Tlingit
Wood, paint, tooth, ferrous nails
19 × 62 × 10 cm
DAC 615

Although this shaman figure and rattle were sold as a set, they were created at different times by different hands. The oral history of these objects asserts that the figure was found inside the carved salmon. Because the story of a shaman traveling in a dream in the belly of salmon is well known, it would not be unusual to see a newer salmon carving made to hold an older sculpture of a shaman for the market. — KAM

Cat. no. 18

SHOT POUCH, c. 1800

Artist unknown, Mesquakie
Hide, quill, glass beads, metal
68.6 × 13 × 1.25 cm
DAC 641

Cat. no. 19

BASKET, c. 1910

Mary Dick Topino (Mrs. Britches),
Wukchumne Yokuts
Deer grass, sedge root, bracken fern
root, redbud
25 × 52 cm
DAC 642

Cat. no. 20

GRASS DANCE MIRROR BOARD, c. 1885

Artist unknown, Omaha
Wood, lead, copper, mirror, ferrous(?)
pins, pigment
35 × 16 × 3 cm
DAC 686

Cat. no. 21

HALIBUT HOOK, c. 1850

Artist unknown, Tlingit
Wood, vegetal fiber, pigment
33 × 6 × 6 cm
DAC 680

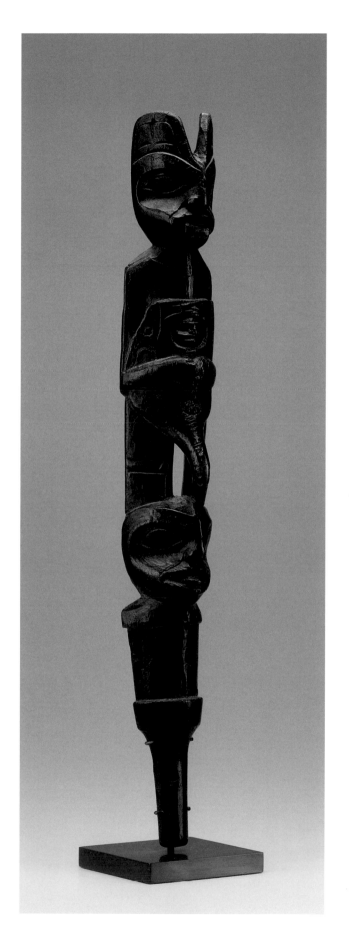

Cat. no. 22
BLANKET STRIP, c. 1865
Artist unknown, Nez Perce(?)
Hide, glass beads, porcupine quill,
copper alloy bells, wool, sinew
15 × 160 × 3 cm
DAC 690

Cat. no. 23
PIPE, c. 1820
Artist unknown, Eastern or Great Lakes
Pipestone, wood
4 × 29 × 2 cm
DAC 721

Cat. no. 24
PIPE, c. 1820
Artist unknown, Eastern
or Great Lakes
Pipestone, wood
4 × 29.5 × 2 cm
DAC 722

Cat. no. 25

HAT, c. 1820

Artist unknown, Maliseet
Cloth, glass beads
17 × 17.5 cm
DAC 724

Cat. no. 26

CADDOS, 1880

Julian Scott Ledger Artist A, Kiowa
Paper, pigment
19.1 × 30.5 cm
DAC 053LD

Emotion

GOOD ART ELICITS *EMOTION* — AN EXPERIENCE OF BEAUTY, OF A moment captured in time, of a piece of light, or of an event represented exactly as you, the observer and appreciator, remember. Objects are beautiful when their combination of materials and ideas enables them to speak to the viewer on an emotional level. Images provide sometimes joy, sometimes an understanding of one's own position in the cosmos.

While the immediacy of the imagery may create this emotion, it can also be created by the realization that a painting or a basket was made by a family member or a recognition of its ties to a cultural or historical event.

Ultimately, emotion is about perfection—a response to the flawless combination of materials, colors, shapes, sizes, and other physical attributes of the artwork that stirs deep within our souls.

Opposite: **Blanket strip,** c. 1830, artist unknown, Upper Missouri or Northern Plains; hide, glass beads, sinew, 26 × 170 × 3 cm, DAC 707 (cat. no. 56). **Raven rattle,** c. 1840, artist unknown, Haida; wood, vegetal wrap, pigment, 12 × 37 × 9 cm, DAC 650 (cat. no. 49). **Kilili katsina figure,** c. 1890, artist unknown, Zuni; wood, cotton fabric, yarn, hide, leather, feathers, hair, paper, metal, shell, nails, cotton thread, grass, pigment, 52 × 16 × 12 cm, DAC 280 (cat. no. 33). This page, background: **Bowl,** c. 1910, artist unknown, Tlingit; spruce root, grasses, 36 × 36 cm, DAC 406 (cat. no. 41).

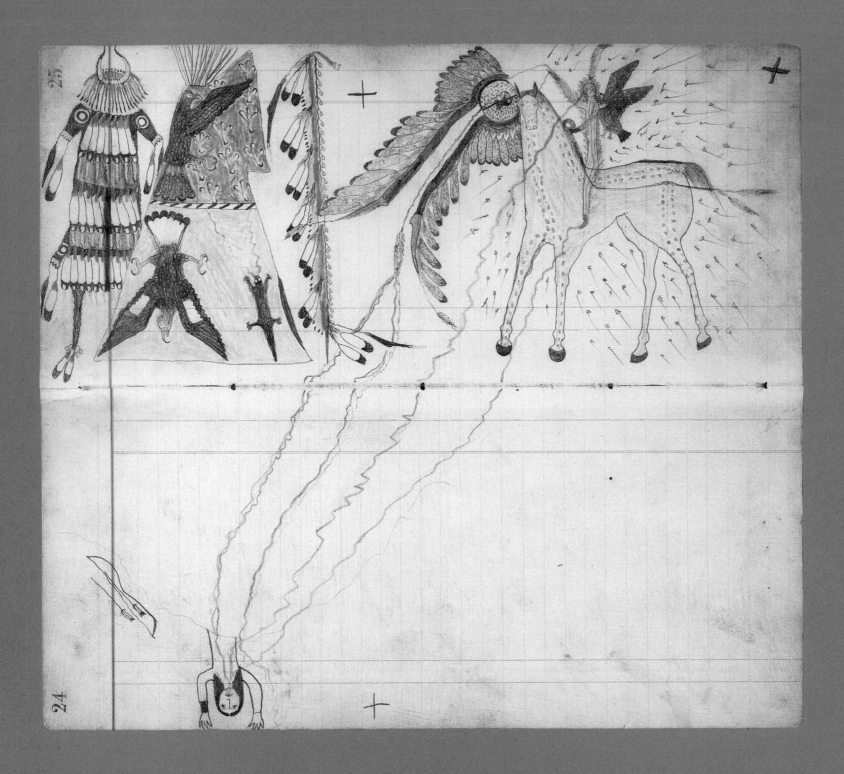

Cat. no. 27

MEDICINE VISION, C. 1882

Henderson Ledger Artist A, Arapaho
Pencil, colored pencil, ink
27 × 30 cm
DAC 024LD

The figure in the bottom half of this image, connected to the upper half by wavy power lines, seems to be somewhere between a dream and a trancelike state. This scene, loaded with haunting imagery, shares expressive qualities with the work of contemporary, so-called outsider artists, yet there is nothing "outsider" about it—in fact, it was expected that all men would live by the power of their dreams. —GM

Cat. no. 28

TOBACCO BAG, c. 1880

Artist unknown, Teton Lakota
Hide, glass beads, quill, ink(?), pigment
100 × 18 × 2 cm
DAC 139

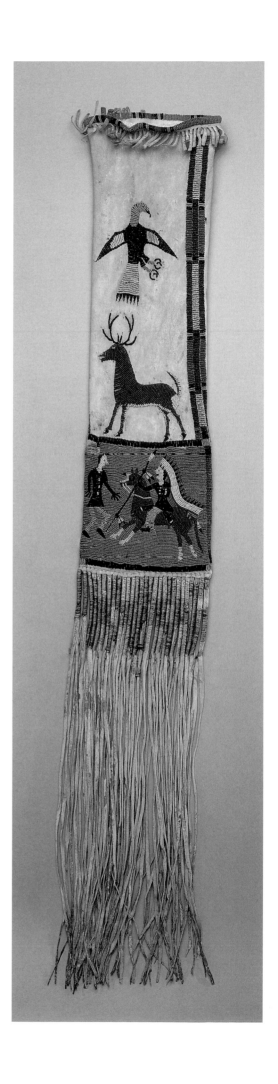

Cat. no. 29

TOBACCO BAG, c. 1860

Artist unknown, Blackfeet
Hide, glass beads, wool, cotton thread,
sinew, pigment (from handling)
109 × 18 × 2 cm
DAC 144

Cat. no. 30
PAHLIK′ MANA KATSINA FIGURE, c. 1890

Artist unknown, Hopi
Wood, feathers, shell, pigment, cordage
41 × 26 × 10 cm
DAC 198

Cat. no. 31
PAIYAKYAMU (CLOWNS), c. 1895

Artist unknown, Hopi
Wood, pigment
51.4 × 7.6 cm
DAC 192

Cat. no. 32

TOBACCO BAG, c. 1870

Artist unknown, Cheyenne
Hide, glass beads, wool, tinned iron,
horsehair, sinew
74 × 17 × 3 cm
DAC 272

Cat. no. 33

KILILI KATSINA FIGURE, c. 1890

Artist unknown, Zuni
Wood, cotton fabric, yarn, hide, leather, feathers, hair,
paper, metal, shell, nails, cotton thread, grass, pigment
52 × 16 × 12 cm
DAC 280

Although made for the non-Zuni art market, this piece nonetheless clearly conveys Zuni history and culture. It was part of
the Throw-Away Dance that would follow a period of warfare.
Because there is no longer warfare in and among the Pueblos,
the dance today is more commonly known as the Harvest Dance,
reflecting the time of the year it is performed. —BB

Cat. no. 34
HANIA KATSINA FIGURE, c. 1890

Artist unknown, Hopi
Wood, cotton, wool, feathers, tinned iron,
hide, pigment
41 × 17 × 14 cm
DAC 317

Cat. no. 35
DOLL, c. 1880

Artist unknown, Mohave
Clay, cotton fabric, cotton cordage,
glass beads, stone, ferrous pin,
cotton thread, slip
20 × 9 × 6 cm
DAC 323

Cat. no. 36
JAR, c. 1790

Artist unknown, Chumash
Sumac, dyed and undyed juncus
17 × 24 cm
DAC 363

Cat. no. 37

TRAY, c. 1880

Artist unknown, Western Apache
Willow, Martynia, cottonwood
10 × 32 cm
DAC 381

Cat. no. 38

TRAY, c. 1930

Lucy Makil, Pima
Cattail, willow shoots, devil's claw
4 × 35 cm
DAC 401

This basket tray aligns the body and mind with the cosmos.
It evokes the emotion associated with highly charged cultural
histories such as the one depicted here, the Man in the Maze,
which tells of the Pima people's origins. — BB

Cat. no. 39
MOCCASINS, c. 1830
Artist unknown, Cherokee
Native-tanned and Native-dyed
hide, glass beads, ribbon
6.4 × 19.4 cm each
DAC 424

Cat. no. 40
MOCCASINS, c. 1880
Artist unknown, Otoe-Missouria
Hide, cotton fabric, glass beads,
cotton thread, sinew
8.5 × 11 × 27 cm each
DAC 433

Cat. no. 41

BOWL, c. 1910

Artist unknown, Tlingit
Spruce root, grasses
36 × 36 cm
DAC 406

The weaver has incorporated her innate understanding of her culture and environment into this piece, although it was made to be sold outside the Tlingit world. While the buyer may have read the piece as a souvenir of Alaska, the whales, which illustrate the supernatural, played a central role in the daily life of the weaver. —BB

Cat. no. 42

PIPE, c. 1860

Artist unknown, Eastern Lakota
Pipestone, lead, wood, brass, cotton,
pigment, brass tacks
12 × 93 × 4 cm
DAC 467

Cat. no. 43
SOUL CATCHER, c. 1850

Artist unknown, Nisga'a, Gitxsan, or Tsimshian(?)
Bone, abalone shell, pigment, hide (thong), cedar
(wadding)
3.5 × 20 × 3.5 cm
DAC 507

Cat. no. 44
SHAMAN'S AMULET, c. 1850

Artist unknown, Tlingit
Bone, pigment
5 × 14 × 3 cm
DAC 508

Cat. no. 45

BANDOLIER BAG, c. 1830

Artist unknown, Seminole
Wool, silk, glass beads, copper alloy,
cotton thread
73 × 46 × 4 cm
DAC 517

Cat. no. 46

MASK, c. 1850

Artist unknown, Tlingit
Wood, pigment
21 × 15 × 10 cm
DAC 545

bottom view

Cat. no. 49

RAVEN RATTLE, c. 1840

Artist unknown, Haida
Wood, vegetal wrap, pigment
12 × 37 × 9 cm
DAC 650

Historically, the Raven rattle was seen from a distance by invited guests at a potlatch. Only a few people were intimate with its form and iconography—the artist who carved it, the chief who owned and danced with it, and the keepers who cared for it. Although they were unable to appreciate the finer details of the carving, the witnesses understood the rattle was a defining object of chiefly power. — PM

Cat. no. 48
CLAPPER, c. 1870

Artist unknown, Coast Tsimshian
Wood, pigment, vegetal cordage, copper wire
10 × 24 × 6 cm
DAC 618

Cat. no. 47

KAMLEIKA, c. 1910

Annie Oktokiyuk, Inuit
Marine mammal intestine, auklet beaks
and feathers, sinew, hide, walrus fur
111.76 × 154.94 × 7.62 cm
DAC 563

Cat. no. 50
WOMAN'S HOOD, c. 1860
Artist unknown, Ojibwe
Silk, wool, glass beads, cotton thread
65 × 27 × 18 cm
DAC 663

Cat. no. 51
COMB, c. 1840
Artist unknown, Tlingit
Horn
13 × 8 × 1.5 cm
DAC 662

Cat. no. 52
BAG, c. 1820
Artist unknown, Great Lakes
Vegetal fiber (hemp?), wool
14 × 20.3 cm
DAC 672

Cat. no. 53

PAHLIK´ MANA KATSINA FIGURE,
c. 1890

Artist unknown, Hopi
Wood, pigment, feathers, cotton cordage
36 × 10 × 6 cm
DAC 682

Cat. no. 54

PAHLIK´ MANA KATSINA FIGURE,
c. 1890

Artist unknown, Hopi
Wood, pigment, cotton thread, feathers
34 × 13 × 8 cm
DAC 683

Cat. no. 55

SHIELD, c. 1885

Joseph No Two Horns, Hunkpapa Lakota
Hide, feathers, pigment, ink, sinew,
cordage, wood
43 × 8 cm
DAC 691

Cat. no. 56
BLANKET STRIP, c. 1830
Artist unknown, Upper Missouri
or Northern Plains
Hide, glass beads, sinew
26 × 170 × 3 cm
DAC 707

One of the most striking and powerful objects in
the Diker collection, the design of this blanket
moves the viewer with its masterful use of only
two colors in large "pony beads." A single red
bead punctuates the beautiful composition.

— KAM

Cat. no. 57

DANCE MASKS, c. 1870

Artist unknown, Alutiiq
Wood, pigment
43 × 25 × 18 cm each
DAC 711

Native American languages are very verb oriented. Similarly, in art it's the process that is really important. For instance, in the making of a mask, the "making" is basically a ritual in itself. —TH

Cat. no. 58

BAG, c. 1800

Artist unknown, Eastern Great Lakes
Hide, porcupine quill, cotton(?) thread
26.7 × 24.1 cm
DAC 715

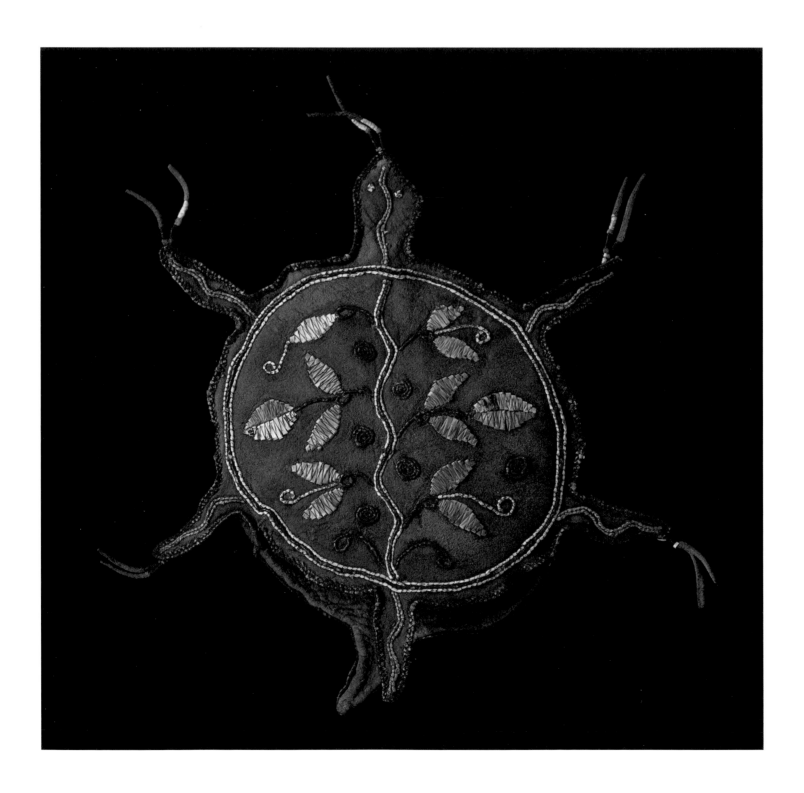

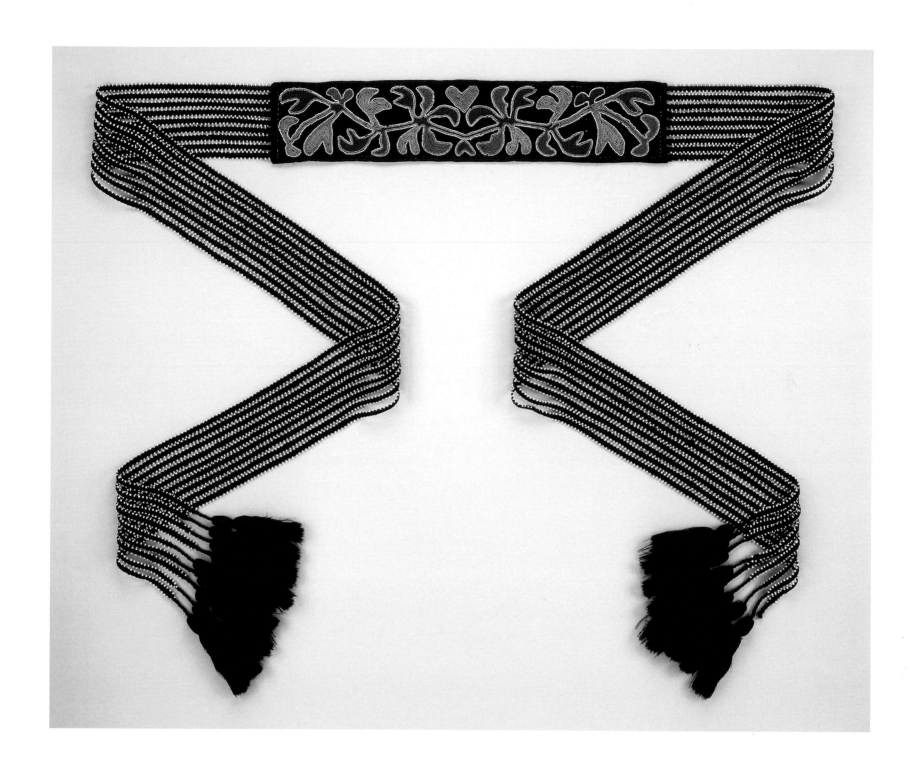

Cat. no. 59

SASH, 1835

Artist unknown, Seminole
Cloth, glass beads
10 × 318 × .5 cm
DAC 723

Intimacy

INTIMACY IS THE PERSONAL NATURE OF NATIVE-MADE ART — THE relationship of the maker and user to the art. Intimacy can come from a lifetime of immersion in the forms, materials, and techniques of art. Cedar, for example, is a familiar and respected material among carvers, part of their natural and spiritual landscapes, ineradicably part of their culture's consciousness.

Most of us are outsiders to indigenous art, whether because we are non-Indian or from a tribe different from the one that created a particular work; a privilege comes from being a relative or fellow tribal member of the maker. Intimacy is this complex of social, cultural, and family relationships that enhance and surround art.

Opposite: **Wives Honoring Husbands**, c. 1880, Julian Scott Ledger Artist, Kiowa; paper, ink, colored pencil, 19 × 32 cm, DAC 047LD (cat. no. 87). **Baby carrier**, c. 1885, artist unknown, Ute; hide, wood, glass beads, wool, feathers, tinned iron, quill, 140 × 55 × 17 cm, DAC 417 (cat. no. 75). This page, background: **Shoulder pouch**, c. 1870, artist unknown, Navajo; commercially tanned leather, glass beads, silver, sinew, 65 × 25 × 6 cm, DAC 458 (cat. no. 74). **Grass Dance whistle**, c. 1870, artist unknown, Lakota; wood, fur, pigment, beads, cotton thread, 76 × 4 × 4 cm, DAC 462 (cat. no. 76).

Cat. no. 60
CHILD'S MOCCASINS,
c. 1880

Artist unknown, Lakota
Hide, glass beads, sinew
6 × 4.5 × 14 cm each
DAC 115

Cat. no. 61
CHILD'S MOCCASINS,
c. 1880

Artist unknown, Lakota
Hide, glass beads, sinew, pigment
7 × 8.5 × 16 cm each
DAC 116

Cat. no. 62
CHILD'S MOCCASINS,
c. 1880

Artist unknown, Arapaho
Hide, glass beads, sinew
6 × 6 × 13 cm each
DAC 118

Cat. no. 63
CHILD'S MOCCASINS,
c. 1880

Artist unknown, Northern Plains
Hide, glass beads, sinew
9 × 5 × 10 cm each
DAC 120

Cat. no. 64

TOBACCO BAG, c. 1860

Artist unknown, Ute
Hide, glass beads, iron, copper,
wood, sinew, cotton thread
89 × 24 cm
DAC 140

Cat. no. 65

BOY'S SHIRT, c. 1875

Artist unknown, Blackfeet
Hide, ermine, glass beads, wool,
metal, mirror, pigment, copper bells,
cotton cloth
60 × 116 × 5 cm
DAC 150

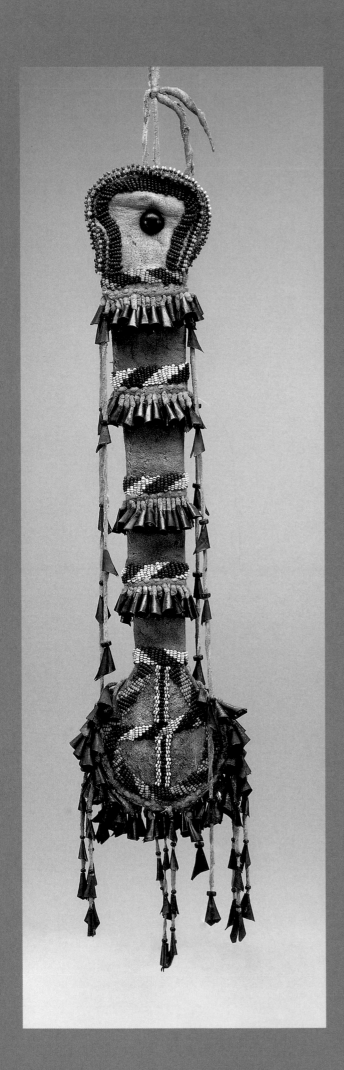

Cat. no. 66

AWL CASE, c. 1860

Artist unknown, Apache
Hide, copper alloy(?) tinklers, glass
beads, "plastic" button, cotton thread,
sinew, pigment
48 × 13 × 4 cm
DAC 173

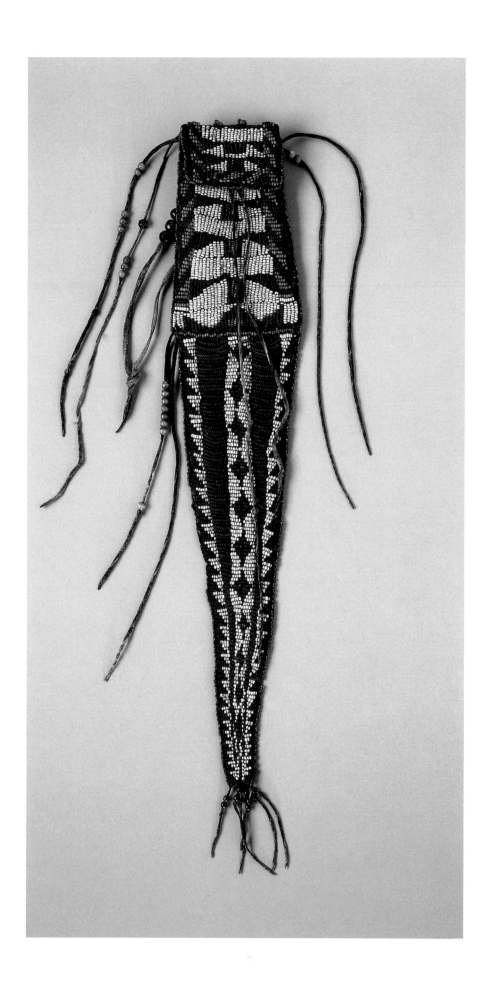

Cat. no. 67
TAIL BAG, c. 1860
Artist unknown, Ute
Leather, hide, glass beads,
copper beads
66 × 11 × 1 cm
DAC 177

Cat. no. 68

CHILD'S MOCCASINS, c. 1880

Artist unknown, Fort Berthold (Hidatsa, Mandan, or Arikara)
Hide, cotton fabric, porcupine quill, cotton thread
4.5 × 5 × 11 cm each
DAC 185

Cat. no. 69

CHILD'S MOCCASINS, c. 1880

Artist unknown, Arapaho
Hide, vegetal-tanned hide, glass beads, sinew, pigment
8 × 7 × 13 cm each
DAC 186

Cat. no. 70
CHILD'S MOCCASINS, c. 1900

Artist unknown, Lakota
Hide, cotton velveteen(?), glass beads,
sinew, cotton thread
6 × 5 × 12 cm each
DAC 187

Cat. no. 71
KAU-A KATSINA FIGURE,
c. 1880

Artist unknown, Hopi
Wood, feathers, cotton cordage
25 × 10 × 6 cm
DAC 321

Cat. no. 72
TOBACCO BAG, c. 1870
Artist unknown, Cheyenne
Hide, cotton, glass beads,
horsehair, tinned iron, sinew
84 × 18 × 5 cm
DAC 251

Cat. no. 73
SHOULDER POUCH, c. 1870
Artist unknown, Navajo
Vegetal-tanned hide, silver, glass
beads, shells, hide
79 × 26 × 4 cm
DAC 457

Cat. no. 74
SHOULDER POUCH, c. 1870
Artist unknown, Navajo
Commercially tanned leather,
glass beads, silver, sinew
65 × 25 × 6 cm
DAC 458

Leather pouches like these were
intimate objects, made to hold
personal items such as a man's
silver-working tools. — KAM

Cat. no. 75

BABY CARRIER, c. 1885

Artist unknown, Ute
Hide, wood, glass beads, wool,
feathers, tinned iron, quill
140 × 55 × 17 cm
DAC 417

Aesthetic sensibilities were extended even to infancy, as a form
of adoration and treasuring. We recognize the universal human
quality of the emotion associated with the intimacy of mother-
hood and punctuate it through precious media. —AA

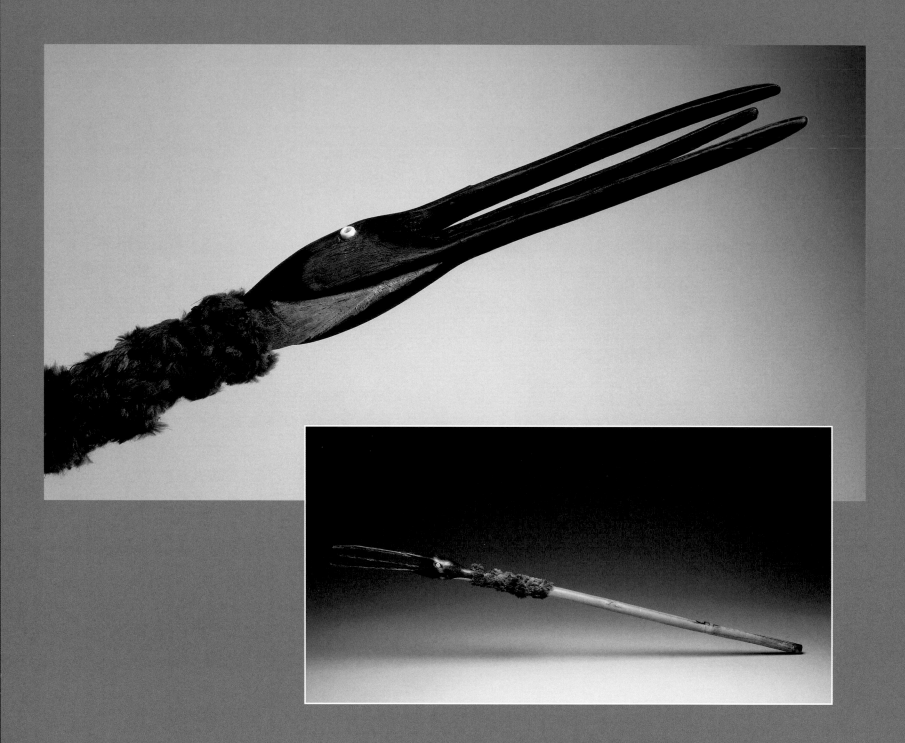

Cat. no. 76
GRASS DANCE WHISTLE, c. 1870
Artist unknown, Lakota
Wood, fur, pigment, glass beads, cotton thread
76 × 4 × 4 cm
DAC 462

Although this whistle was used in a social dance, it was the
person holding and playing the instrument who was most able
to enjoy the beauty and grace in the carver's rendition of the
bird. — KAM

Cat. no. 77
SOAPBERRY SPOON, c. 1885

Artist unknown, Tlingit
Wood, pigment
46 × 5 × 2.5 cm
DAC 509

Cat. no. 78

SIFTING TRAY, c. 1920

Amanda Wilson, Maidu
Sedge root, briar root, willow
1 × 39.5 cm
DAC 518

Cat. no. 79
BOWL, c. 1860

Artist unknown, Pomo
Sedge root, bulrush root, willow,
glass beads, feathers
13 × 25 cm
DAC 519

Cat. no. 80
JAR, c. 1910

Mary Winkle, Panamint-Shoshone
Joshua-tree root, dyed juncus, sumac
19 × 27 cm
DAC 520

Cat. no. 81

BOWL, c. 1750

Artist unknown, Eastern Great Lakes
Wood
11 × 16 cm
DAC 566

Cat. no. 82

TREASURE BASKET, c. 1900

Artist unknown, Aleut, Atka Island
Beach grass, split bird quills, wool yarn
19 × 16 cm
DAC 579

Cat. no. 83
KNIFE AND SHEATH,
c. 1790

Artist unknown, Eastern
Great Lakes
Hide, quill, iron, cotton thread,
tinned iron, horsehair
48 × 7 × 8 cm
DAC 585

Cat. no. 84

BATTLE OF THE LITTLE BIGHORN, c. 1920

Standing Bear, Lakota
Cotton, ink, pencil, watercolor
96 × 265 cm
DAC 652

This piece was done by my great-grandfather. His name was
Standing Bear. He was born in 1859 and fought in the Battle of
the Little Bighorn on June 25, 1876. As members of the Crazy
Horse band, which surrendered in 1877, his family lived in a
marginal situation on the Pine Ridge reservation. In 1887, and
from 1889 to 1890, he traveled and performed with the Buffalo
Bill Wild West Show in Europe, where he was left behind for two
years because he was injured. He met and married a Viennese
upper-class woman who returned with him to the reservation as
his wife and marketer. —AA

Cat. no. 85

CHILD'S MOCCASINS, c. 1875

Artist unknown, Lakota
Hide, quill, glass beads, sinew
7 × 8 × 13 cm each
DAC 699

Cat. no. 86

CROOKED KNIFE, c. 1840

Artist unknown, Algonquin Mocotaugan(?),
possibly Delaware
Wood, steel, shellac
33 × 4 × 2 cm
DAC 725

This is a very personal piece. The knife is incredibly beautiful yet utilitarian. It was used for splitting and trimming basketry materials and other wood. The decorative grip adds nothing to the piece's functionality, yet without the designs carved into the handle, the knife would neither "feel" nor work right. The artwork is also private, with no one but the user aware of the decoration when it is held in the hand to be used. Even the user would need to stop using the piece in order to admire the artistry of the handle. —BB

Cat. no. 87

WIVES HONORING HUSBANDS, C. 1880

Julian Scott Ledger Artist, Kiowa
Paper, ink, colored pencil
19 × 32 cm
DAC 047LD

Ledger drawings, private iterations of the artist's view of the world done in books, exude a sense of intimacy. This drawing, which represents a public ceremony celebrating intimacy in marriage, once came from a book, evidence of which is seen in the ragged edges and the page number. —GM

Cat. no. 88

**TWELVE HIGH-RANKING KIOWA
MEN,** c. 1880

Julian Scott Ledger Artist B, Kiowa
Paper, ink, colored pencil
18.5 × 31 cm
DAC 059LD

Movement

NATIVE ART IS MADE TO EXPRESS *MOVEMENT* THROUGH PATTERN, shape, or symbol. This movement refers not only to the dynamism of the immediate physical environment but also to the universe that surrounds us, from the sky above us to the earth beneath our feet. It is evident in the pattern of winding plants on a basket or the vibrating beadwork designs on a bag, in a dress worn, a mask danced with, a strike-a-light bag carried and used.

Creation is part of the present for Native people rather than an historic event. The making of art is part of the continuing creation of the world. This sense of the world as being in constant motion is like the fringe on a woman's buckskin dress or the jingles on a powwow dancer's outfit, which sway and leap to life with the wearer's movement.

Aesthetic anticipation of an object's kinetic existence—that it is to be worn, folded, or thrown over the shoulder, for example—is part of the making of the object. Movement is an integral characteristic of the object's relationship to its user.

Opposite and this page, background (left to right): **Moccasins,** c. 1875, artist unknown, Assiniboine; hide, cotton fabric, glass beads, cotton thread, 12 × 10 × 43 cm each, DAC 285 (cat. no. 149). **Moccasins,** c. 1870, artist unknown, Kiowa; hide, glass beads, sinew, pigment, 10 × 9 × 48 cm each, DAC 104 (cat. no. 89). **Child's moccasins,** c. 1880, artist unknown, Arapaho; hide, glass beads, sinew, 6 × 6 × 13 cm each, DAC 118 (cat. no. 62). **Moccasins,** c. 1850, artist unknown, Iroquois; hide, moose hair, porcupine quill, silk, glass beads, cotton thread, 9 × 8 × 25 cm each, DAC 483 (cat. no. 130). **Child's moccasins,** c. 1875, artist unknown, Lakota; hide, quill, glass beads, sinew, 7 × 8 × 13 cm each, DAC 699 (cat. no. 85). **Child's moccasins,** c. 1880, artist unknown, Lakota; hide, glass beads, sinew, 6 × 4.5 × 14 cm each, DAC 115 (cat. no. 60). **Moccasins,** c. 1875, artist unknown, Lakota; hide, parfleche, porcupine quill, horsehair, tinned iron, glass beads, fabric, 12 × 11 × 26 cm each, DAC 551 (cat. no. 135).

Cat. no. 89

MOCCASINS, c. 1870

Artist unknown, Kiowa
Hide, glass beads, sinew, pigment
10 × 9 × 48 cm each
DAC 104

Cat. no. 90

BLANKET STRIP, c. 1880

Artist unknown, Kiowa
Hide, glass beads, cotton thread
19 × 158 × 1 cm
DAC 159

It is impossible to fully appreciate the aesthetic impact of Plains clothing without seeing it in motion. The continuously active fringes of moccasins like these swayed and dragged, drawing the eye back and forth in a visually stunning movement. — KAM

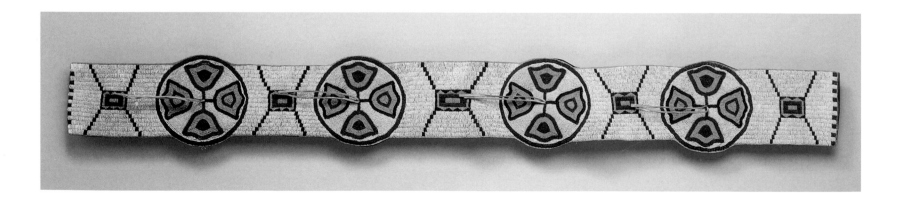

Cat. no. 91
CANE, c. 1850
Artist unknown, Woodlands culture
Wood, ferrous screw, ferrous nails, pigment
92 × 8 × 8 cm
DAC 189

The man depicted on this cane has climbed a limb
to evade a ferocious serpent from whom there is
no other escape. The image evokes the condition
of the cane's owner, a person who is similarly
inconvenienced. —GM

Cat. no. 93

CHIEF KILLER AT A TURKEY SHOOT,
1876–78

Chief Killer, Cheyenne
Paper, pencil, ink, crayon
22 × 28.6 cm
DAC 205LD

Cat. no. 94

MIRROR BAG, c. 1885

Artist unknown, Nez Perce
Hide, wool, cotton quill,
copper alloy
60 × 16 × 6 cm
DAC 242

Cat. no. 95

DISPATCH CASE, c. 1870

Artist unknown, Kiowa
Vegetal-tanned leather, cotton
cordage, glass beads, dye, pigment,
cotton thread
61 × 20 × 3 cm
DAC 253

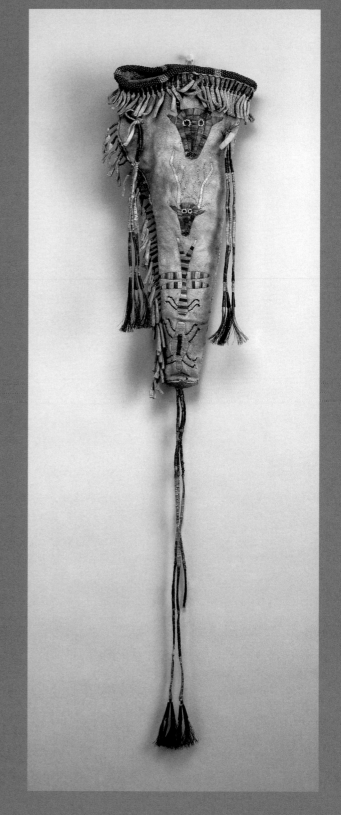

Cat. no. 96

REVOLVER HOLSTER,
c. 1870

Artist unknown, Eastern Lakota
Hide, quill, glass thread, tinned
iron, horsehair
67 × 18 × 7 cm
DAC 250

Cat. no. 97

MOCCASINS, c. 1875

Artist unknown, Kiowa
Hide, glass beads, tinned iron,
wool, pigment, cotton thread
9 × 10 × 43 cm each
DAC 281

Cat. no. 98

MOCCASINS, c. 1880

Artist unknown, Kiowa
Hide, glass beads, pigment, cotton
thread, sinew
9 × 11 × 37 cm each
DAC 288

Cat. no. 99

TRAY, c. 1890

Artist unknown, Western Apache
Willow, cottonwood, Martynia
11 × 54 cm
DAC 395

Cat. no. 100

BOWL, c. 1880

Artist unknown, Central Pomo
Sedge root, willow, glass beads,
abalone shells
12 × 25 cm
DAC 396

Cat. no. 101

BOY'S SHIRT, c. 1880

Artist unknown, Crow
Hide, wool, sinew, cotton thread
59 × 120 × 3 cm
DAC 415

The stark, graphic quality of the beadwork design on this shirt belies the sense of movement and changing boundaries it would have when worn across the body of an active boy. — KAM

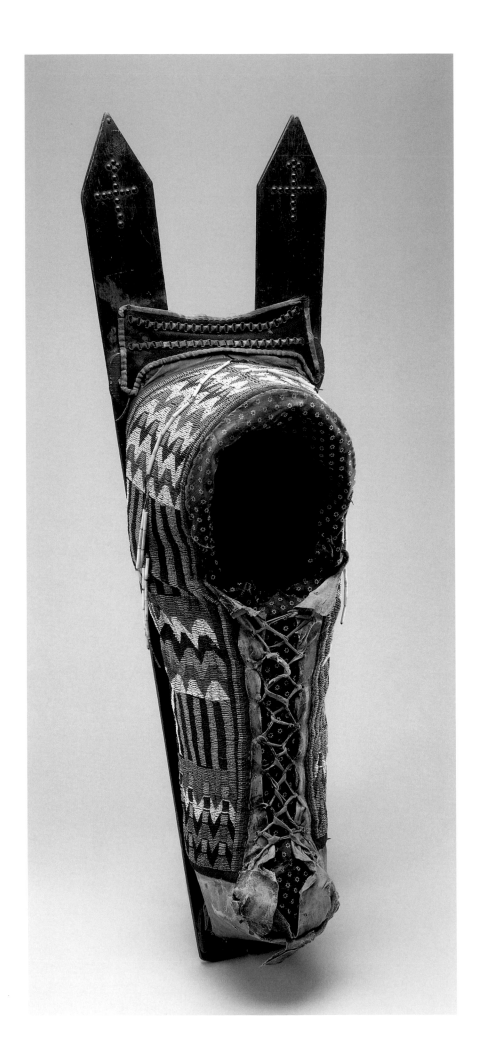

Cat. no. 102

BABY CARRIER, c. 1870

Artist unknown, Kiowa
Hide, wood, cotton fabric, glass beads,
copper alloy (brass), iron, cotton thread
110 × 34 × 25 cm
DAC 416

The baby carrier is a dynamic object meant to be seen
from several viewpoints, including that of the child held
in its protective swaddling and that of the observer watch-
ing it in motion on a mother's back. —KAM

Cat. no. 103

DRESS, BELT, AND AWL,
c. 1870

Artist unknown, Wasco
Hide, glass beads, teeth, shell, sinew,
thimbles, vegetal-tanned hide (belt),
brass
Dress: 150 × 138 × 5 cm
DAC 459

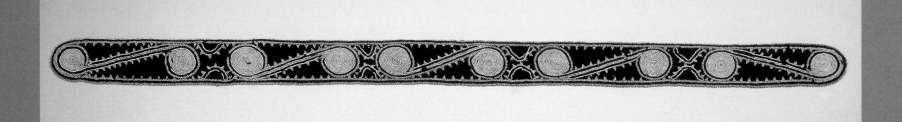

Cat. no. 104

SASH, 1780–1800

Artist unknown, Choctaw
Wool, glass beads, cordage
9 × 144 × .5 cm
DAC 500

We can appreciate the elegant beadwork design of this vibrant
sash in its stationary state. In use, the sash would have been
part of a visually active ensemble, tied to the wearer, swaying
to and fro. — KAM

Cat. no. 105

MOCCASINS, c. 1830

Artist unknown, Creek
Hide, glass beads, silk, cotton thread
10 × 8 × 26 cm each
DAC 542

Cat. no. 106

CEREMONIAL DANCE ORNAMENT,
c. 1900

Artist unknown, Yup'ik
Wood, feathers, pigment
26.8 × 91.8 cm
DAC 526

Cat. no. 107

BOWL, c. 1910

Artist unknown,
Mountain Maidu
Redbud, bracken
fern root, willow
15 × 25 cm
DAC 587

Cat. no. 109

DRESS, c. 1870

Artist unknown, Lakota
Native-tanned hide, sinew,
glass beads
116.8 × 88.9 × 6.4 cm
DAC 572

Cat. no. 108

LIDDED STORAGE JAR,
c. 1890

Mrs. Reese, Karuk
Conifer root, bear grass,
maidenhair fern stems,
hazel sticks
33 × 29 cm
DAC 596

Cat. no. 110

CAPE, c. 1800

Artist unknown, Tlingit
Hide, pigment, sinew
102 × 68 × 2 cm
DAC 645

Cat. no. 111

SHIRT, c. 1890

Artist unknown, Nez Perce
Hide, quill, horsehair, wool,
glass beads, pigment
154 × 83 cm
DAC 666

Cat. no. 112
RATTLE, c. 1780
Artist unknown, Tsimshian
Wood, hair, bone, nails, pigment,
sinew, rattling material
37 × 20 × 14 cm
DAC 664

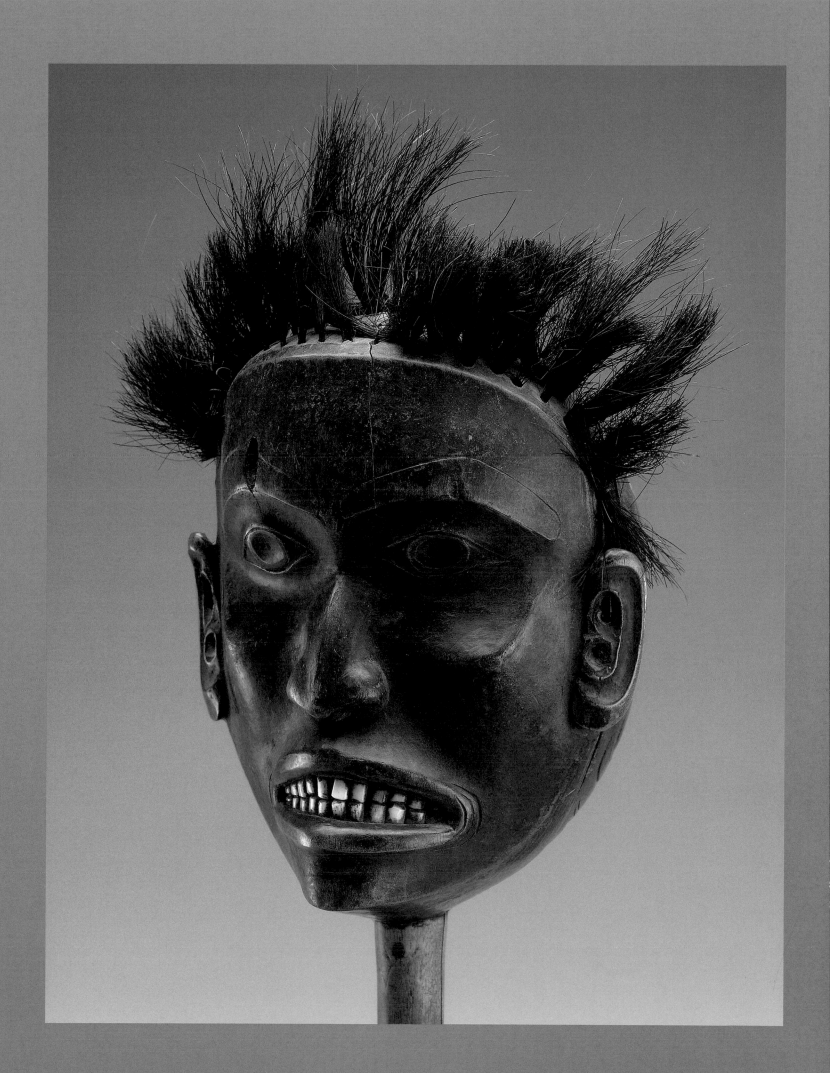

Cat. no. 113
CLAPPER, c. 1870
Artist unknown, Heiltsuk
Wood, hide, pigment, nails, hair
22 × 41 × 9 cm
DAC 679

bottom view

Cat. no. 114
STRIKE-A-LIGHT,
c. 1880

Artist unknown, Kiowa
Leather, hide, tinned iron, glass
beads, bone, metal beads, sinew
33 × 10 × 1.5 cm
DAC 692

Cat. no. 115
STRIKE-A-LIGHT,
c. 1880

Artist unknown, Kiowa
Leather, hide, tinned iron,
glass beads, shell, sinew
26 × 12 × 4 cm
DAC 693

Cat. no. 116
STRIKE-A-LIGHT,
c. 1880

Artist unknown, Kiowa
Leather, hide, copper alloy,
glass beads
45 × 12 × 5 cm
DAC 695

Cat. no. 117

STRIKE-A-LIGHT,
c. 1880

Artist unknown, Kiowa
Leather, hide, tinned iron,
silver, glass beads, sinew
36 × 13 × 8 cm
DAC 696

Cat. no. 118

STRIKE-A-LIGHT,
c. 1880

Artist unknown, Kiowa
Leather, hide, glass beads,
bone, tinned iron, silver,
copper alloy, sinew
42 × 13 × 5 cm
DAC 697

Cat. no. 119

SALLY BAG, c. 1900

Artist unknown, Wasco
Native hemp, corn husks
30 × 17.5 cm
DAC 719

Integrity

***INTEGRITY* IS WHAT A CULTURE USES TO ACHIEVE BALANCE AS IT** embraces its past while incorporating new materials and ideas. Artists are keen observers, shaping new ideas into existing patterns as well as shaping new patterns from old ideas, keeping art fresh and alive through the tension between the known and the unknown. They make the relationship between the old and the new material accessible.

New influences and markets have long been part of Native art, but that art has also remained true to its origins; this is evidenced in pieces that remain tribal in spirit although the ideas and materials might be international. Integrity was crucial to the process of fusing old with new in the transformation of Native cultural traditions in the twentieth century, when Indian people were the subject of tourism and were sentimentalized by non-Indians.

Integrity guides the character of individuals as artists and their relationship to cultural heritage over time, the human and more-than-human worlds around them, their traditional media, and the level of mastery they must reach in order to articulate both form and idea.

Opposite: ***Swift Dog in Pursuit of a Mounted Crow Warrior,*** c. 1870, Swift Dog, Hunkpapa Lakota; paper, ink, watercolor, 21 × 34 cm, DAC 169LD (cat. no. 121). ***Octopus bag,*** c. 1860, artist unknown, St. James Bay Cree; cotton, wool, silk, glass beads, wood, cotton thread, 59 × 30 cm, DAC 689 (cat. no. 141). ***Tea cozy,*** c. 1850, artist unknown, Mi'kmaq; velvet, silk, glass beads, cotton thread, 33 × 46 × 4 cm, DAC 464 (not illustrated elsewhere). ***Olla,*** 1919–20, Maria and Julian Martinez, San Ildefonso Pueblo; clay, slip, 29 × 35 cm, DAC 305 (cat. no. 123). ***Dogfish frontlet,*** c. 1860, artist unknown, Haida; wood, paint, abalone, 20 × 16 × 5 cm, DAC 540 (cat. no. 136). This page, background: reverse image.

Cat. no. 120

SHIRT, c. 1880

Artist unknown, Crow
Hide, ermine, glass beads, wool, hair,
feathers, cotton fabric, cotton thread
120 × 144 cm
DAC 152

Cat. no. 121

SWIFT DOG IN PURSUIT OF A MOUNTED CROW WARRIOR, c. 1870

Swift Dog, Hunkpapa Lakota
Paper, ink, watercolor
21 × 34 cm
DAC 169LD

Cat. no. 122

WOMAN'S HOOD, c. 1875

Artist unknown, Mi'kmaq
Wool, silk, glass beads, cotton thread
39 × 22 × 3 cm
DAC 279

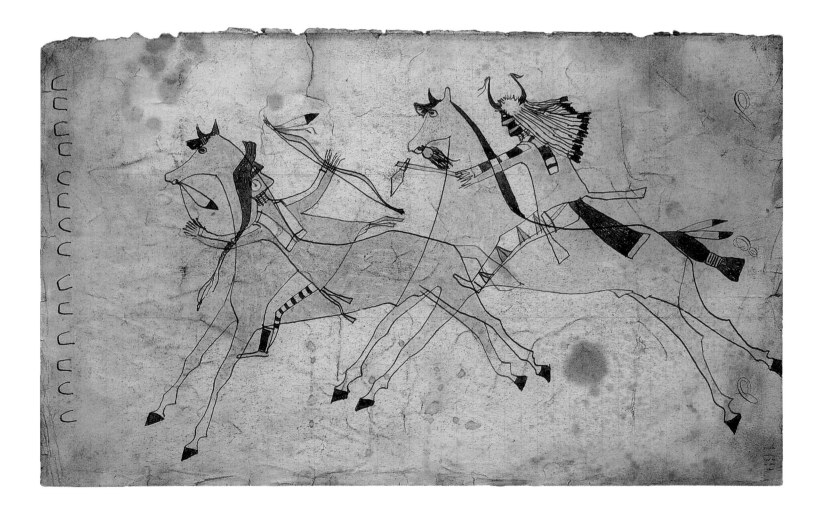

Cat. no. 123

OLLA, 1919–20

Maria and Julian Martinez, San Ildefonso Pueblo
Clay, slip
29 × 35 cm
DAC 305

This piece represents the creative artistry and technological
excellence of perhaps the most important American Indian
artists of the twentieth century. In the winter of 1919–20,
Maria and Julian Martinez created this new type of pottery
based on an existing form, decorating it with an innovative
technique as well as new iconography. —BB

Cat. no. 124
JAR, c. 1895
Nampeyo, Hopi
Clay, slip
19 × 33 cm
DAC 311

Nampeyo's name and family today are cultural icons of Pueblo
pottery. Nampeyo was a remarkable person, who revived a
300-year-old ancestral potting tradition through the reinter-
pretation of shapes, designs, and clays. Although the style she
created—today known as the Sikyatki revival—is part of a long
potting tradition, it is an art movement in and of itself, not just
a re-creation of an ancestral style of pottery. —BB

Cat. no. 125
OLLA, c. 1910

Artist unknown, Panamint or
Chemehuevi, Victorville,
California
Willow, Martynia, juncus
14 × 18 cm
DAC 346

Cat. no. 126
OLLA, c. 1920

Annie Poole, Miwok/Paiute
Sedge, redbud, bracken fern root
19 × 22 cm
DAC 354

Cat. no. 127

SHOULDERED JAR, c. 1912

Lucy Telles, Miwok/Paiute
Sedge, redbud, bracken fern root
12 × 25 cm
DAC 356

Cat. no. 128
PLATE, c. 1885
Artist unknown, Maidu
Redbud, willow
5 × 35 cm
DAC 384

Cat. no. 129
LADLE, c. 1840
Artist unknown, Menomini
Wood, white metal (silver?)
26 × 12 × 14 cm
DAC 466

Cat. no. 130
MOCCASINS, c. 1850
Artist unknown, Iroquois
Hide, moose hair, porcupine quill,
silk, glass beads, cotton thread
9 × 8 × 25 cm each
DAC 483

Cat. no. 131

COAT AND TROUSERS, c. 1850

Artist unknown, Métis
Hide, porcupine quill, bone, copper, silver tassels, wool
Coat: 43.2 × 171.5 cm; trousers: 78.7 × 78.7 cm (waist circumference)
DAC 492

The Métis, a unique culture resulting from a cross between
Cree and French cultures, flourished in the Red River area of
Manitoba. In this work we see this fusion in the highly tailored
coat and trousers with a porcupine-decorated smoked moose
hide. Traditional fringes along the trouser leg are similar to
those on Plains-style leggings. —GM

Cat. no. 132

RATTLE, c. 1840

Artist unknown, Tlingit
Wood, paint, black and red pigment,
cedar root, pebbles
12 × 21.6 × 7.62 cm
DAC 512

Cat. no. 133

PIPE, c. 1780

Artist unknown, Eastern Woodlands
Wood, metal (lead?), ferrous nails(?)
9.5 × 18 × 8 cm
DAC 531

The artistic tradition of carving is well known in the Eastern
Woodlands. In this relatively realistic work, a male figure
grasps his chest. His head, from which a pipe bowl springs, is
thrust upward in a seemingly impossible position. Countless
references to smoking during this period make it clear that the
practice was ubiquitous. It is difficult to tell whether this bowl
was used for personal pleasure or in ceremonial situations.

— GM

Cat. no. 134
SHOT POUCH, c. 1760

Artist unknown, Western Ojibwe
Hide, porcupine quill, vegetal fiber cordage,
tinned iron, wool, cotton thread
54 × 21 × 6 cm
DAC 532

I like the idea of quillwork and different-colored quills making
block-like designs. Those sorts of block-like abstract designs are
seen in many decorative arts of the world. —JB

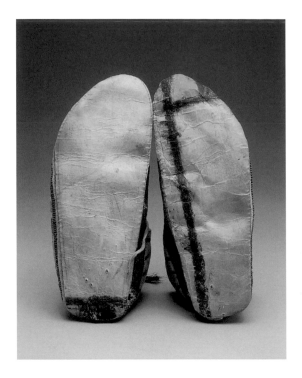

Cat. no. 136

DOGFISH FRONTLET, c. 1860

Artist unknown, Haida
Wood, paint, abalone
20 × 16 × 5 cm
DAC 540

Wood is not like other materials; like quill or clay, it has its own set of challenges. [An artist] can do something in wood that can't be done in silver because one medium has grain and one does not. With its plastic quality, this front-let seems almost to go beyond wood. — RD

Cat. no. 135

MOCCASINS, c. 1875

Artist unknown, Lakota
Hide, parfleche, porcupine
quill, horsehair, tinned iron,
glass beads, fabric
12 × 11 × 26 cm each
DAC 551

Cat. no. 137
KNIFE CASE, c. 1870
Artist unknown, Eastern Lakota
Hide, porcupine quill, tinned iron,
wool, glass beads, cotton thread
27 × 8 × 4 cm
DAC 552

Cat. no. 138
TREASURE BOWL, c. 1850
Artist unknown, Plains Miwok
Sedge root, willow, beads, feathers
15 × 25 cm
DAC 594

Cat. no. 139
GREASE DISH, c. 1830
Artist unknown, Haida
Alder
7.62 × 25.4 × 7.62 cm
DAC 644

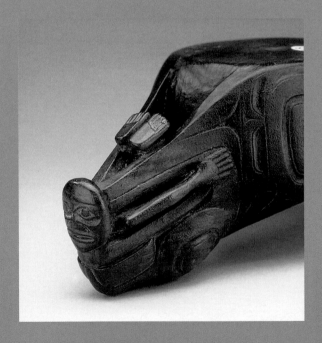

bottom view

bottom view

Cat. no. 140

RATTLE, c. 1850

Artist unknown, Tsimshian
Wood, shell, sinew(?), paint
13 × 28 × 10 cm
DAC 671

Cat. no. 141

OCTOPUS BAG, c. 1860

Artist unknown, St. James Bay Cree
Cotton, wool, silk, glass beads, wood, cotton thread
59 × 30 cm
DAC 689

The artist took a chance with this bag in giving it five tabs rather
than the traditional four, thus redefining the idea of symmetry.

— AM

Cat. no. 142

BOWL, c. 1890

Artist unknown, Tlingit
Wood, shell, pigment
30 × 32 × 16 cm
DAC 703

Cat. no. 143

MASKETTE, c. 1840

Artist unknown, Tsimshian or Tlingit(?)
Wood, copper, shell, pigment
18 × 15 × 9 cm
DAC 681

Vocabulary

JUST AS PROSPECTIVE ARTISTS MUST KNOW THE FORMAL PRINCIPLES of art—form, line, texture, and so on—before they can manipulate or control their media, they must also learn a cultural *vocabulary*. Vocabulary expresses the knowledge, origins, and consciousness encoded in materials, techniques, and iconography. It is a culture's way of understanding and giving meaning to the environment—the sum total of its history, predictable or unpredictable, strange or well known.

Vocabulary is as straightforward as the materials and techniques chosen and as meaningful as the realization that the art is a physical manifestation of creation. The work of an artist is not only form and mass but also an element of cultural genesis, a profound and direct connection to ancestors, past, present, and future.

Opposite: *Olla,* c. 1790, artist unknown, Tewa; clay, slip, 44 × 42 cm, DAC 307 (cat. no. 152). *Lidded jar,* c. 1910, Elizabeth Conrad Hickox, Karuk; hazel shoots, conifer root, maidenhair fern stem, bear grass, 19 × 23 cm, DAC 445 (cat. no. 158). *Horn spoon,* c. 1850, artist unknown, Haida; horn, shell, copper, 28 × 8 × 26 cm, DAC 506 (cat. no. 162). *Baby moccasins,* c. 1875, artist unknown, Plains (Lakota?); hide, porcupine quill, glass beads, cotton thread, 6 × 7 × 13 cm each, DAC 581 (cat. no. 167). This page, background: reverse image.

Cat. no. 144

GIRL'S DRESS, c. 1885

Artist unknown, Teton Lakota
Hide, glass beads, copper alloy beads, sinew
93 × 70 × 3 cm
DAC 154

Cat. no. 145

MOCCASINS, c. 1880

Artist unknown, Crow
Hide, glass beads, tinned iron,
wool, sinew, cotton thread
10.5 × 11 × 26 cm each
DAC 114

Cat. no. 146

OLLA, c. 1890

Artist unknown, Laguna
Clay, slip
26 × 28 cm
DAC 221

Cat. no. 147

GAUNTLETS, c. 1910

Artist unknown, Plateau
Hide, cotton fabric, glass and metal beads,
cotton thread, silk
36 × 28 × 4 cm each
DAC 276

The Nez Perce and other Plateau tribes embraced the horse culture of Plains tribes during the nineteenth century. Although these gauntlets reflect the influence of the European-American cowboy style, they are made indigenous by the fringe and imagery. Nez Perce identity is often associated with the raising of Appaloosa horses, and in this image we see the mottled rump of such a horse. Unlike the self-directed designs seen on moccasins, this imagery is intended for an external viewer. —GM

Cat. no. 148
PARFLECHES, c. 1880
Artist unknown, Blackfeet
Rawhide, pigment
38 × 25 cm each
DAC 269

Cat. no. 149

MOCCASINS, c. 1875

Artist unknown, Assiniboine
Hide, cotton fabric, glass beads, cotton thread
12 × 10 × 43 cm each
DAC 285

Cat. no. 150

MOCCASINS, c. 1870

Artist unknown, Cheyenne
Hide, glass beads, sinew, pigment,
cotton thread
8 × 10 × 25 cm each
DAC 284

Cat. no. 151

MOCCASINS, c. 1885

Artist unknown, Plains Cree
Hide, cotton fabric, glass beads,
metal beads, cotton thread
10 × 9 × 27 cm each
DAC 291

Cat. no. 152

OLLA, c. 1790

Artist unknown, Tewa
Clay, slip
44 × 42 cm
DAC 307

Large jars are difficult to make. The side walls will collapse on themselves if the clay is too wet or crack between the coils if the clay is too dry. Pueblo pottery is made using the coil-and-scrape method. The designs symbolize the relationship of Pueblo people to water and fertility. —BB

Cat. no. 153

OLLA, c. 1880

Artist unknown, Apache
Willow, Martynia, yucca root
55 × 47 cm
DAC 409

Cat. no. 154

BOWL, c. 1790

Artist unknown, Chumash
Dyed and undyed juncus, sumac
11 × 37 cm
DAC 383

Cat. no. 155

JAR, c. 1880

Artist unknown, Tubatulabal
Yucca, Martynia, sumac,
willow, feathers
16 × 28 cm
DAC 362

Cat. no. 156

JAR, c. 1880

Artist unknown, Tubatulabal
Sedge root, bracken fern root,
yucca root, sumac, willow
13.6 × 22 cm
DAC 357

Cat. no. 157

KNIFE CASE, c. 1870

Artist unknown, Cheyenne
Rawhide, hide, tinned iron, glass beads, sinew
38 × 8 × 4 cm
DAC 413

Cat. no. 158

LIDDED JAR, c. 1910

Elizabeth Conrad Hickox, Karuk
Hazel shoots, conifer root, maidenhair
fern stem, bear grass
19 × 23 cm
DAC 445

Elizabeth Hickox was able to master her art with more skill than
any other Karuk or other basket weaver from the northwestern
California region. Her work perfectly embodies a combination
of materials, technique, and design; even her stitches are sized to
complement the elegant forms. She worked full-time as an artist,
her family serving as her assistants by preparing her materials.

— BB

Cat. no. 159
BABY CARRIER, c. 1880

Artist unknown, Comanche
Hide, wool, cotton fabric, copper tacks,
cotton thread, pigment
106 × 29 × 23 cm
DAC 499

Cat. no. 160
MAN'S SUMMER COAT, c. 1840

Artist unknown, Innu
Hide, pigment
65 × 109 × 12 cm
DAC 490

Cat. no. 161

FINIAL OR DOWN CUP, c. 1840

Artist unknown, Haida
Bone or tusk(?), abalone shell, pigment(?)
14 × 6 × 4 cm
DAC 504

bottom view

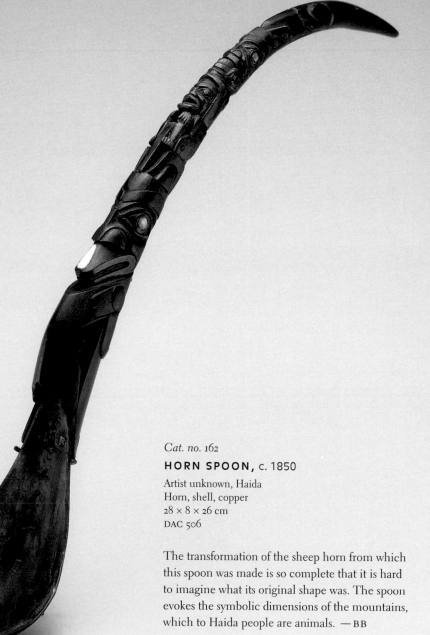

Cat. no. 162

HORN SPOON, c. 1850

Artist unknown, Haida
Horn, shell, copper
28 × 8 × 26 cm
DAC 506

The transformation of the sheep horn from which
this spoon was made is so complete that it is hard
to imagine what its original shape was. The spoon
evokes the symbolic dimensions of the mountains,
which to Haida people are animals. — BB

Cat. no. 163

HORSEWHIP (QUIRT) HANDLE, c. 1860

Artist unknown, Mesquakie
Bone, paint
38 × 5 × 6 cm
DAC 513

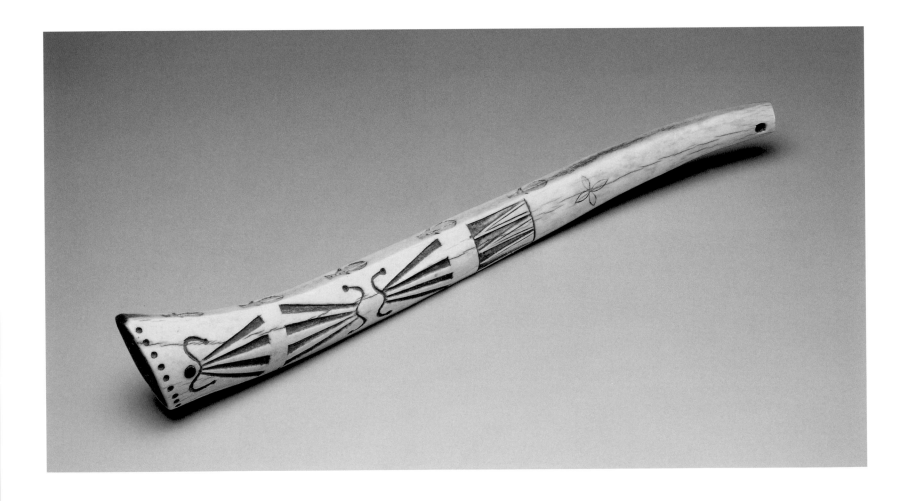

Cat. no. 164

BELT CUP, c. 1820

Artist unknown, Eastern Woodlands
Wood, nail, lead(?), staple
16 × 9 × 5 cm
DAC 515

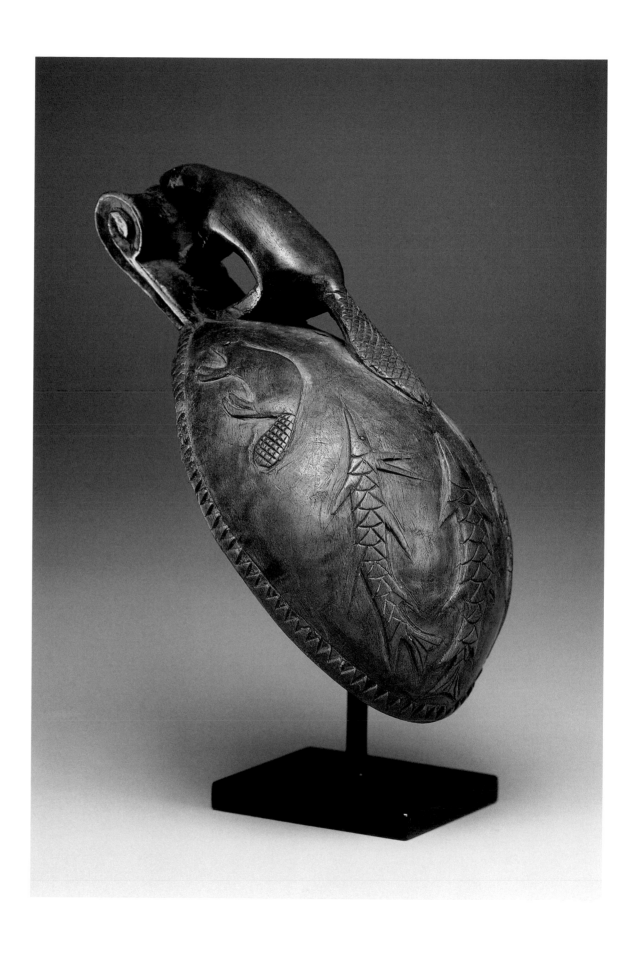

Cat. no. 165

GIFT BASKET, c. 1890

Mary Mona, Southern Pomo
Clamshell, glass beads, quail topknot
feathers, sedge root
10 × 19 cm
DAC 523

Cat. no. 166

BOWL, c. 1790

Artist unknown, Tlingit
Wood, shell
18 × 29 cm
DAC 544

Cat. no. 167

BABY MOCCASINS,
c. 1875

Artist unknown, Plains (Lakota?)
Hide, porcupine quill, glass beads,
cotton thread
6 × 7 × 13 cm each
DAC 581

Cat. no. 168
BAG, c. 1860
Artist unknown, Wasco
Cotton fabric, cotton thread, glass beads,
hide, copper alloy buttons, beads
74 × 18 × 5 cm
DAC 570

Cat. no. 169
BOY'S SHIRT, c. 1870
Artist unknown, Arapaho
Hide, sinew, glass beads
52 × 52 × 7 cm
DAC 631

Cat. no. 170
DAGGER, c. 1750

Artist unknown, Tlingit(?)
Iron, hair, cordage, hide, wool
48 × 12 × 4 cm
DAC 610

Among the Tlingit of northern British Columbia
and southern Alaska, warrior art such as this dagger is associated with rich stories. In this piece,
what may be one solid piece of metal connects
both the blade and the pommel with the hilt,
which is wrapped in protective material. The
pommel is made in repoussé style, the face star-
ing at us contorted and grimacing as if it is being
throttled. —GM

Cat. no. 171
KNIFE SHEATH, c. 1860

Artist unknown, Cree
Hide, glass beads, silk, cotton, cotton thread
44 × 18 × 2 cm
DAC 653

Cat. no. 172
BAG, c. 1860
Artist unknown, Delaware(?)
Silk, wool, cotton, glass beads, cotton thread
37 × 19 × 2 cm
DAC 710

Cat. no. 173
CAP, c. 1860
Artist unknown, Canadian
Delaware(?)
Hide, porcupine quill, cotton(?)
thread, sequin
18 × 23 × 14 cm
DAC 712

This cap is a fine example of
Northeastern beadwork. The
presence of sequins often indicates an Iroquois influence,
suggesting that the cap is from
Ontario, where the Delawares
lived alongside the Iroquois at
Six Nations and other locales.

—AM

Cat. no. 174
BOWL, c. 1900
Artist unknown, Tlingit
Spruce root, beach grass
10.5 × 11.4 cm
DAC 717

21
Kiowa
Muscallero Apache,
One of Victoria's band!

Cat. no. 175

KIOWA VANQUISHING NAVAJO,
c. 1880

Julian Scott Ledger Artist (see cat. no. 87), Kiowa
Paper, ink, colored pencil
19 × 31 cm
DAC 021LD

Composition

COMPOSITION REACHES BEYOND MATERIAL FORM TO A HIGHER consciousness. The purposefulness of the universe, in which every plant and animal has cultural attributes and meanings, is embodied in art through the proper combination of elements of a visual vocabulary. Composition is like a language, with its own grammatical rules of comprehension and expression that are contained within cultural frameworks of language, philosophy, identity, and history.

Composition is the physical and spiritual putting together of a piece through the combination of technique and materials. It is what makes us gasp at the beauty of a basket flawlessly created from thousands of evenly colored and sized stitches in a perfect fusion of materials, design, and shape. Through this aesthetic harmony, composition conveys intellectual notions of order, emotional states of happiness, physical states of health, and moral conditions.

The making of art is, for Native cultures, the act of making beauty as well as the act of creation itself. The production of art helps maintain the world's equilibrium and, when necessary, serves as a correction. The finished composition is a by-product of the continued creation of the world.

Opposite: **Presentation bowl,** 1907, Datsolalee, Washoe; willow, redbud, bracken fern root, 40 × 40 cm, DAC 326 (cat. no. 187). **Shot pouch,** c. 1855, artist unknown, Métis; hide, porcupine quill, pigment, thread (cotton?), 26 × 17 × 3 cm, DAC 496 (cat. no. 198). **Bandolier bag,** c. 1820, artist unknown, Creek; wool, silk, glass beads, silk, cotton thread, bag: 45 × 22 × 2 cm, strap: 156 × 10 × .5 cm, DAC 533 (cat. no. 200). This page, background: **Jar,** c. 1050, artist unknown, Ancestral Pueblo; clay, slip, 35 × 40 cm, DAC 313 (cat. no. 186). **Bandolier bag,** c. 1830, artist unknown, Creek; wool, cotton, glass beads, silk, cotton thread, 79 × 32 × 9 cm, DAC 576 (cat. no. 203).

Cat. no. 176
MOCCASINS, c. 1895
Artist unknown, Arapaho
Hide, glass beads, sinew, pigment
12 × 10 × 29 cm each
DAC 101

Cat. no. 177
MOCCASINS, c. 1890
Artist unknown, Cree or Métis
Hide, silk, cotton
12 × 17 × 27 cm each
DAC 133

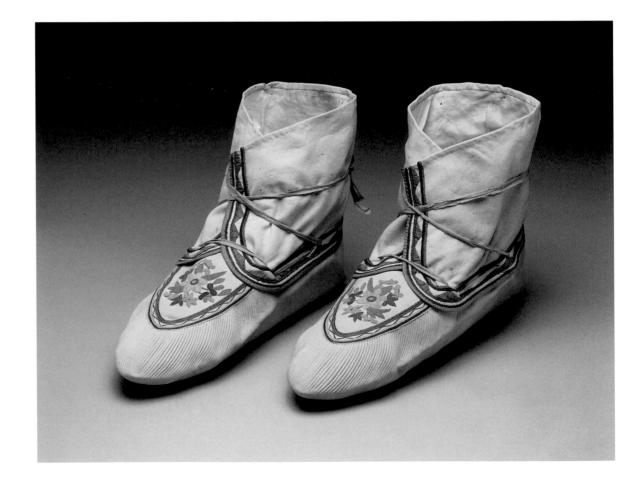

Cat. no. 178

SHOULDER BAG (SHOT POUCH),
c. 1860

Artist unknown, Tahltan
Wool, cotton, glass beads, cotton thread
81 × 23 × 5 cm
DAC 169

Cat. no. 179
BELT POUCH AND AWL CASE, c. 1870

Artist unknown, Kiowa
Vegetal-tanned leather, hide, glass beads, tinned iron,
pigment, silver, sinew
34 × 11 × 6 cm
DAC 175

Cat. no. 180

FINGER-WOVEN SASH, c. 1850

Artist unknown, Great Lakes
Cotton, wool, glass beads
27.5 × 190 × 1 cm
DAC 259

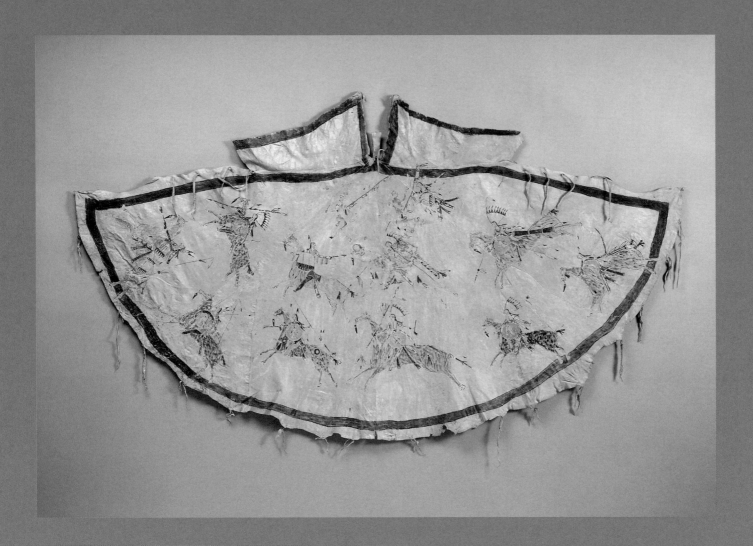

Cat. no. 181
TIPI MODEL, c. 1880
Artist unknown, Teton Lakota
Native-tanned hide, pigment
96.5 × 167.6 cm
DAC 265

Cat. no. 182

SADDLE BAGS, c. 1880

Artist unknown, Lakota
Hide, cotton, glass beads, cotton
thread, tinklers, horsehair
36 × 52 × 7 cm each
DAC 270

It is often noted that women were the abstract artists among the Sioux tribes. The artist who made this pair of bags laid new material upon hide to create glittering work, which, when seen from a distance, creates a lasting impression. Sometimes known as "possible bags"—used to store clothing and other possible stuff—these bags, which were draped, one on each side, over the back of a horse, both complimented and complemented the woman who rode on horseback. Their abstract designs provided careful balance with the world around. —GM

Cat. no. 183

MOCCASINS, c. 1890

Artist unknown, Northern Plains
Hide, glass beads, cotton fabric, pigment
12 × 9 × 27 cm each
DAC 290

Cat. no. 184

MOCCASINS, c. 1920

Artist unknown, Potawatomi
Hide, glass beads, cotton fabric,
cotton thread
7 × 8 × 23 cm each
DAC 293

Cat. no. 185
BOWL, c. 1850
Artist unknown, Haida
Horn, lead(?)
14 × 25 × 12 cm
DAC 300

Cat. no. 186

JAR, c. 1050

Artist unknown, Ancestral Pueblo
Clay, slip
35 × 40 cm
DAC 313

Without focusing on precision or symmetry, the artist created a vibrant and lively design in black and white. Bringing further life to this vessel is a repeat motif that may be a hand or a feather. — KAM, JJB

Cat. no. 187

PRESENTATION BOWL, 1907

Datsolalee, Washoe
Willow, redbud, bracken fern root
40 × 40 cm
DAC 326

Cat. no. 188

PRESENTATION BOWL, c. 1904

Lizzy Toby Peters, Washoe
Willow, redbud, bracken fern root
18 × 28 cm
DAC 359

Cat. no. 189

BOWL, c. 1890

Artist unknown, Pomo
Sedge root, bulrush root, willow,
feathers, clamshell beads
10.5 × 19 cm
DAC 373

Cat. no. 190

HAT, c. 1830

Artist unknown, Tlingit
Spruce root, shell, ermine,
glass beads, pigment, cotton
thread, hide
18 × 34 cm
DAC 389

Cat. no. 191

OLLA, c. 1885

Artist unknown, Chemehuevi
Willow, Martynia
33 × 38 cm
DAC 412

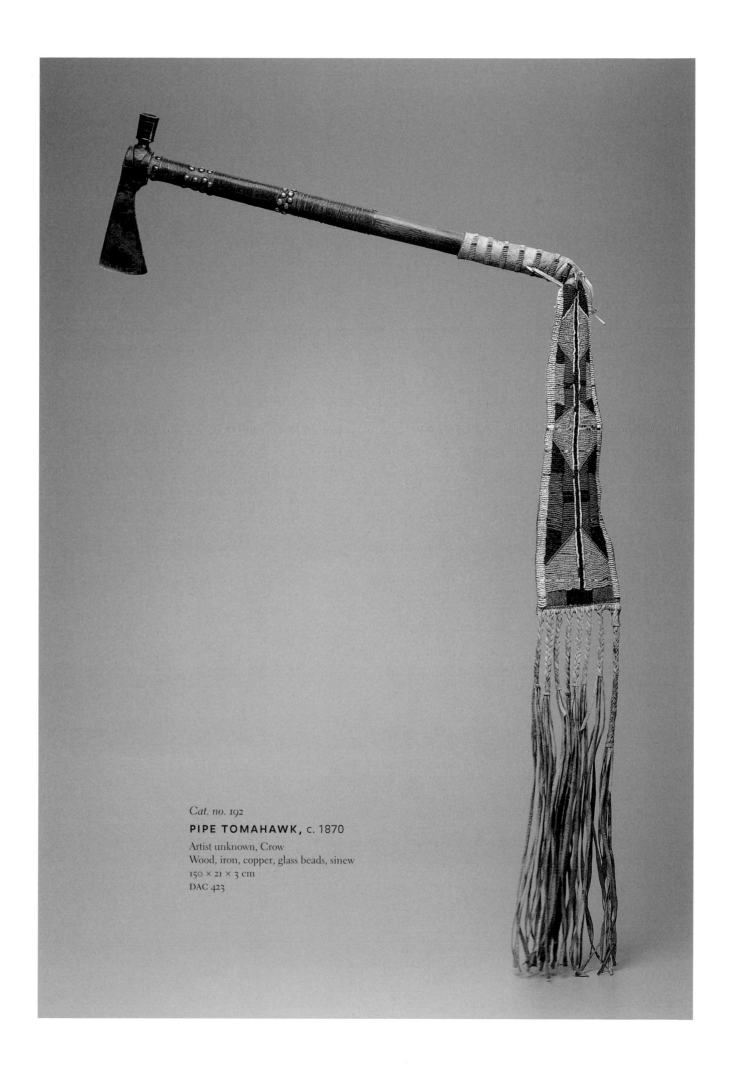

Cat. no. 192
PIPE TOMAHAWK, c. 1870

Artist unknown, Crow
Wood, iron, copper, glass beads, sinew
150 × 21 × 3 cm
DAC 423

Cat. no. 193
MOCCASINS, c. 1860
Artist unknown, Mescalero Apache
Hide, cotton, glass beads, brass,
cotton thread, pigment
13 × 10 × 40 cm each
DAC 434

Cat. no. 194

MOCCASINS, c. 1890

Artist unknown, Crow
Hide, glass beads, cotton fabric,
sinew, cotton thread, pigment
11 × 10 × 28 cm each
DAC 450

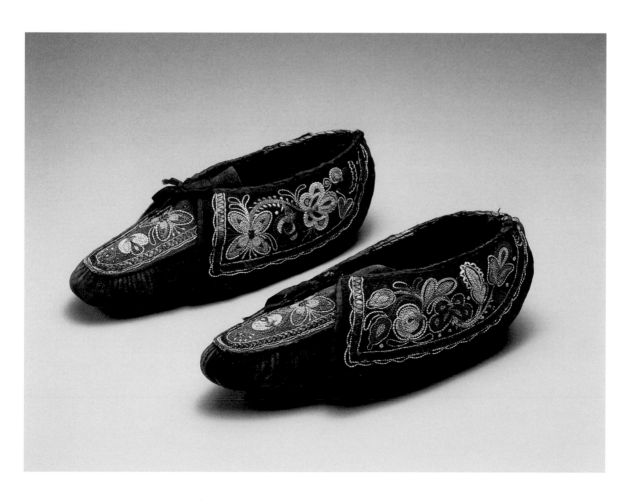

Cat. no. 195

MOCCASINS, c. 1830

Artist unknown, Huron
Hide, quill, silk, moose hair
12 × 10 × 25 cm each
DAC 491

Cat. no. 196
SADDLE, c. 1890

Artist unknown, Plains Cree
Hide, rawhide, cotton, iron, copper,
glass beads, cotton thread
50 × 73 × 6 cm
DAC 442

Cat. no. 197
BABY CARRIER, c. 1885
Artist unknown, Crow
Hide, wool, cotton
114 × 27 × 17 cm
DAC 479

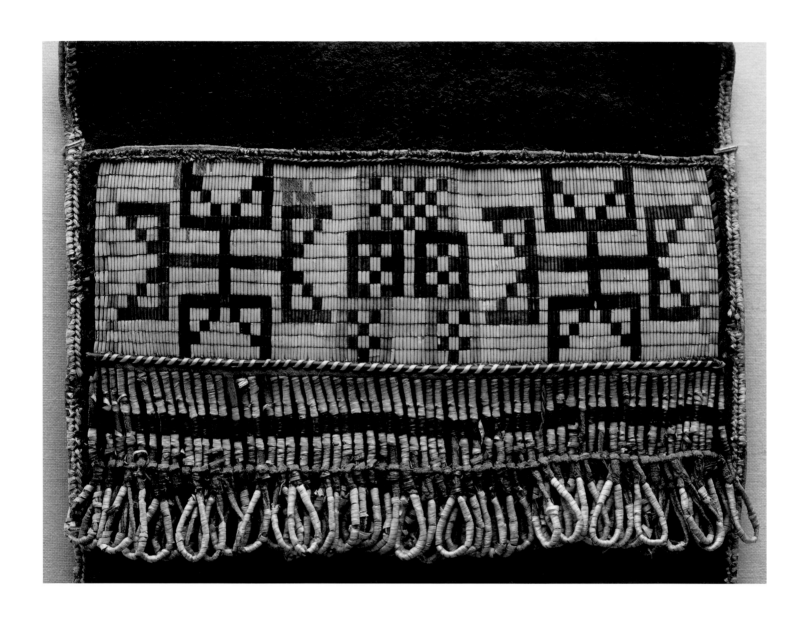

Cat. no. 198

SHOT POUCH, c. 1855

Artist unknown, Métis
Hide, porcupine quill, pigment, thread (cotton?)
26 × 17 × 3 cm
DAC 496

Small objects like this pouch, intimate and interactive,
are meant to be handled and seen up close. —KAM

Cat. no. 199

LADLE, c. 1850

Artist unknown, Chinook
Wood, paint
22 × 16 × 7 cm
DAC 514

This remarkable wooden ladle has a striking silhouette, demonstrating the artist's mastery of sculptural form.

— KAM

Cat. no. 200

BANDOLIER BAG, c. 1820

Artist unknown, Creek
Wool, silk, glass beads, silk, cotton thread
Bag: 45 × 22 × 2 cm; strap: 156 × 10 × .5 cm
DAC 533

Cat. no. 201

MOCCASINS, c. 1850

Artist unknown, Creek
Hide, silk, glass beads, metal beads, cotton thread
13 × 10 × 27 cm each
DAC 534

Cat. no. 202

MAN'S COAT, c. 1840

Artist unknown, Delaware or Shawnee
Hide, glass beads, cotton thread, iron,
cotton fabric
103 × 90 × 10 cm
DAC 535

Cat. no. 203
BANDOLIER BAG, c. 1830

Artist unknown, Creek
Wool, cotton, glass beads, silk,
cotton thread
79 × 32 × 9 cm
DAC 576

Cat. no. 204
BOY'S SHIRT, c. 1885

Artist unknown, Crow
Hide, glass beads, cotton fabric,
wool cloth, sinew, cotton thread
54 × 80 × 1.5 cm
DAC 665

Cat. no. 205

BOWL, c. 1925

Carrie Bethel, Mono Lake Paiute
Sedge root, redbud, bracken fern
root, willow
24 × 52 cm
DAC 706

Cat. no. 206

WOMAN'S HOOD, c. 1850

Artist unknown, Ojibwe
Wool, cotton, glass beads, cotton thread
64 × 26 × 28 cm
DAC 708

Cat. no. 207

PARFLECHES, c. 1890

Artist unknown, Lakota
Rawhide, glass beads, pigment
68 × 33.7 × 8 cm each
DAC 716

Materials and technique are fundamental to a Native aesthetic.
The unlikely combination of colors and of rawhide and glass
beads and the genius required to manipulate these media gave
rise to the sheer beauty of these pieces. — BB

Cat. no. 208

PAWNEE VILLAGE, 1875–78

Fort Marion Ledger Artist, Southern Plains
(Kiowa or Cheyenne)
Paper, ink, pencil, crayon or colored pencil
22 × 28 cm
DAC 018LD

Index

Photos and figures are indicated with **bold** type. Special caption information is indicated with the letter "c," e.g., 157c.

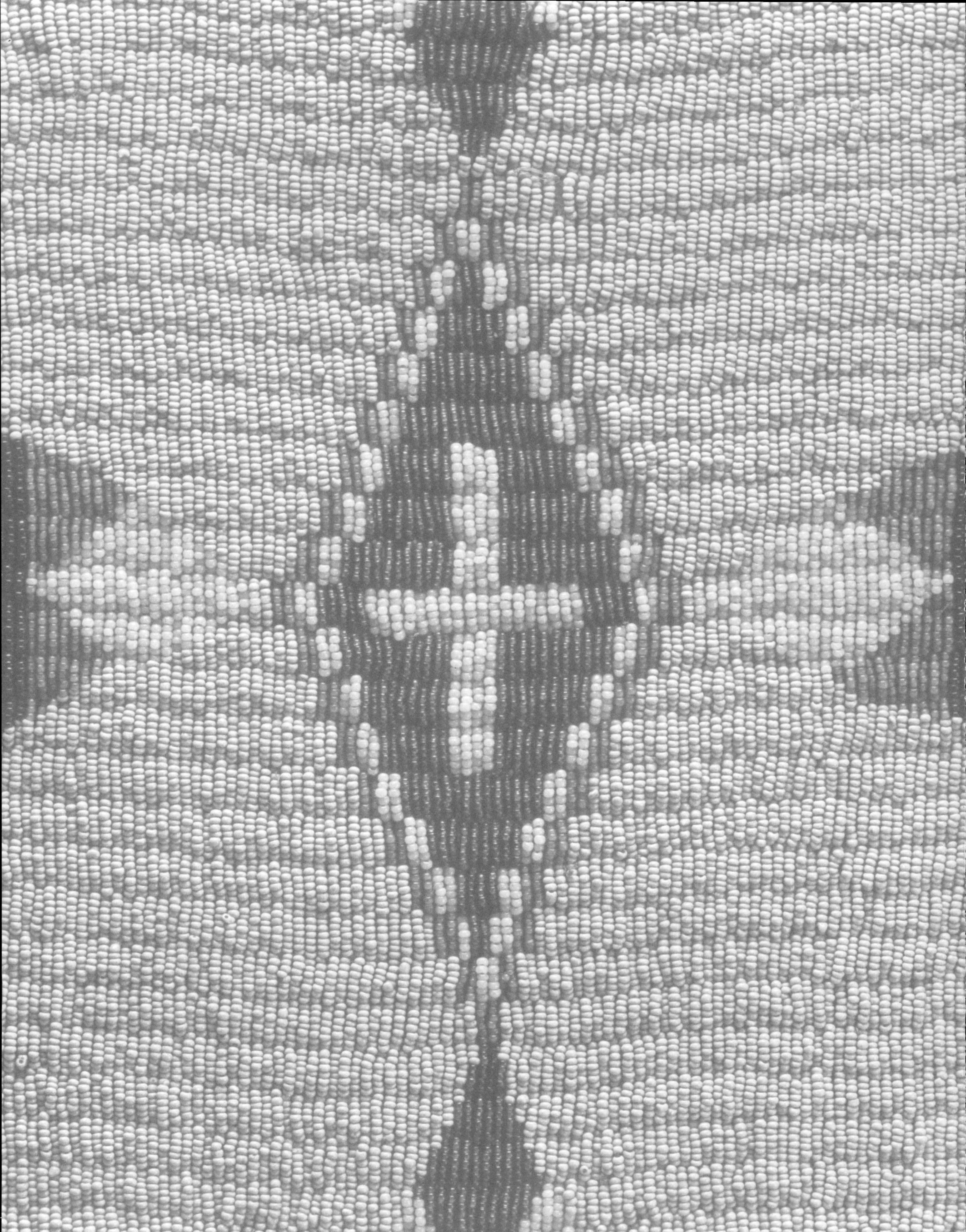